# Praise for *Break Free from Reactive Parenting*

"At last, a parenting book with practical, pragmatic, and proactive strategies that we can actually use and that actually work! Thank you, Laura Linn Knight for creating this beautiful guide that allows us to be the parents we always wanted to be."
—Christopher Willard, author of *Growing Up Mindful* and *Alphabreaths*

"Dear frustrated parents, this book is really good medicine. It has wisdom and humor and honesty that will help, calming your heart and inspiring your best parenting."
—Jack Kornfield, PhD, author of *A Path with Heart*

"As a leader in the mental health industry, I am aware of how important mindfulness and self-regulation are for mental wellness. *Break Free from Reactive Parenting* offers all parents invaluable tools and practical information that is easy to implement and promotes well-being in the home. Laura Linn Knight teaches parents to stop parenting through emotions, which can often escalate a problem and cause more stress for both the child and the parent. Laura has a wealth of knowledge about parent/child relationships of all ages, and the information in this book is instrumental towards creating a more peaceful and loving environment in the home."
—Laura DeCook, founder of LDC Wellbeing and mental health leader

"Laura Linn Knight's book offers all the practical mindfulness tools that stressed-out parents need right now. Practical, nonjudgmental, warm, and compassionate. It's an accessible guide for navigating this wild, beautiful thing we call parenting."
—Sean Fargo, founder of Mindfulness Exercises

T0017976

# BREAK FREE
## FROM
# REACTIVE PARENTING

GENTLE-PARENTING TIPS,
SELF-REGULATION STRATEGIES,
AND KID-FRIENDLY ACTIVITIES FOR
CREATING A CALM AND HAPPY HOME

**LAURA LINN KNIGHT**

*To my family, whose love is a gift beyond words.*
*Thank you for all the laughter, kindness, and compassion you have*
*brought into my life. And to my sweet grandmother, Judy, whose*
*eyes sparkle each time we talk about writing. Thank you, Grandma,*
*for your unwavering encouragement.*

Published by:
Ulysses Press
PO Box 3440
Berkeley, CA 94703
www.ulyssespress.com

ISBN: 978-1-64604-404-7
Library of Congress Control Number: 2022936243

Printed in the United States by Versa Press
10 9 8 7 6 5 4 3 2

Acquisitions editor: Kierra Sondereker
Managing editor: Claire Chun
Project editor: Renee Rutledge
Proofreader: Beret Olsen
Front cover design: Amy King
Cover artwork: © NotionPic/shutterstock.com
Production: Winnie Liu
Illustrations: Alex J. Holguin—page 28; page 53
Images: from shutterstock.com—cover © NotionPic; pages 18, 49, 89 © grayjay; page 90 © All Medical Media; pages 202, 203 © Maquiladora; page 206 © Liliya Krasnova

# CONTENTS

INTRODUCTION ........................................................1

**SECTION 1: COMMON PARENTING PROBLEMS & SOLUTIONS** ................................................... 9

## CHAPTER 1
## USING SELF-REGULATION TO REDEFINE THE WAY YOU PARENT ..................................................... 10

The Keystone of
Self-Regulation ...........................13

Reflection .....................................15

Tool #1: Plan-to-Pause
Poster...........................................17

Tool #2: Favorite Calming
Quotes ..........................................22

Tool #3: Daily Writing
Reflections ...................................23

Tool #4: The Dos and
Don'ts of Self-Regulation........25

FOR YOUR KIDS .....................26

Tool #1: Plan-to-Pause
Poster...........................................29

Tool #2: Big Belly Breaths........31

Tool #3: Seven Wonderful
Picture Books to Read .............32

Tool #4: When You're
Mad—Breathe with the Big
Bad Wolf ......................................32

Tool #5: Coloring Pages
to Help Chill Out .......................33

## CHAPTER 2
## WHO HAS THE POWER? ................................................35

What Is a Power Struggle?.....36

Tool #1: Morning Routine.........37

Tool #2: Calming Cards........... 40

Tool #3: The 3 P's: Problem-
Solve, Plan, Patience............... 43

Tool #4: Order Less and
Ask More...................................... 45

Tool #5: Empathy through
Storytelling................................. 46

Power Struggle Journal.......... 48

FOR YOUR KIDS .....................49

Tool #1: Kids Calming
Cards............................................. 50

Tool #2: Flower-Petal Trick.....52

Tool #3: Mini Gathering ......... 54

Tool #4: Write or Draw
It Out.............................................55

Tool #5: Offer or Ask
for a Hug......................................56

**CHAPTER 3**

## THE GOLDEN CHILD ...................................................57

Tool #1: Fair Treatment ...........58

Tool #2: Be Present ..................65

Tool #3: Special
One-on-One Time......................65

Tool #4: Play Together as
a Family.....................................67

FOR YOUR KIDS ...................... 71

Tool #1: Plan Playtime..............72

Tool #2: Create a Project
Together.....................................73

Tool #3: Kindness Box..............74

Tool #4: Five Awesome
Picture Books.............................75

**CHAPTER 4**

## WORRY IS NOT YOUR FRIEND ...........................76

Tool #1: Dot Activity .................78

Tool #2: Write It Out and
Rip It Up....................................79

Tool #3: Get to the Root ........80

Tool #4: Positive
Affirmations..............................82

Tool #5: Releasing Fears:
Guided Meditation....................85

FOR YOUR KIDS ...................... 87

Tool #1: What Do You See,
Hear, Smell, and Feel?..............88

Tool #2: Name the Worry........88

Tool #3: Big Breaths .................91

Tool #4: Practice and Then
Practice Again...........................92

Tool #5: Changing the
Movie in Your Mind...................93

**CHAPTER 5**

## WEAPONS OF MASS DISTRACTION.............................95

Tool #1: Examining Your
Relationship with Screens ..... 96

Tool #2: Understand the
Research ................................. 99

Tool #3: Awareness of Your
Actions .................................101

Tool #4: Healthy Ways to
Increase Dopamine .................102

Tool #5: Beware of the
Compare-and-Despair
Trap...........................................104

Tool #6: Screen Time for
Kids!..........................................107

Tool #7: Screen-Time Tool
Review .....................................116

FOR YOUR KIDS ......................118

Tool #1: Imagine You Were
the Adult....................................118

Tool #2: Positives and
Negatives of Screen Time.....120

Tool #3: Four Tips to
Balance Screen Time...............121

## CHAPTER 6
## IT'S ALL NEGATIVE SELF-TALK ................................. 123

Tool #1: Contrary
Thoughts..................................... 125

Tool #2: One Kind Act
Each Day..................................... 128

Tool #3: Daily Journal
Prompts.....................................130

Tool #4: Fourteen of My
Favorite Books.......................... 132

FOR YOUR KIDS ....................133

Tool #1: Be Clear with Your
Words............................................134

Tool #2: Daily Reflection:
What Do You Like about
Yourself? ..................................... 136

Tool #3: What Do You Do
When You Make a Mistake?.. 136

Tool #4: Kindness Counts:
One Kind Act Each Day......... 137

## CHAPTER 7
## DID YOU HEAR WHAT I SAID? ........................................140

Tool #1: What's My Part?
And Contrary Actions! ...........142

Tool #2: Order Less, Ask
More, and Offer a Choice!.....145

Tool #3: Getting Down
to Eye Level ...............................147

Tool #4: Create Routines ......149

FOR YOUR KIDS ....................151

Tool #1: Listening Games....... 152

Tool #2: Mindful-Listening
Meditation .................................. 155

Tool #3: Making a
Rain Stick.....................................156

Tool #4: Audiobooks and
Podcasts for Kids.....................158

Tool #5: Story Games.............160

## CHAPTER 8
## IT'S TOOL TIME! ............................................................. 162

Toolbox for You ......................... 163

Toolbox for Your Child...........164

**SECTION 2: CREATE MEANINGFUL CHANGE** .................. 165

## CHAPTER 9
## MIND-FULL TO MINDFUL ............................ 166

Tool #1: Understand the
Myths of Meditation ............... 167

Tool #2: Cultivating Your
Meditation Practice ................ 170

Tool #3: Guided
Meditation ................................. 171

Tool #4: Mindfulness for
Daily Living ............................... 173

Tool #5: Six Mindfulness
Practices ..................................... 177

FOR YOUR KIDS .................... 183

Mindfulness .............................. 183

Tool #1: Mindful Body
Scan ............................................ 184

Tool #2: Mindful Breath ......... 187

Tool #3: Mindful-Alien
Eating ......................................... 188

Tool #4: Mindful Walking ...... 189

Tool #5: Meditation ................ 189

## CHAPTER 10
## HOW TO START AND END YOUR DAY ........................ 192

Tool #1: Carve Out Time
Each Morning for
Meditation ................................. 193

Tool #2: Morning Quiet
Reflection with Journal
Prompt ........................................ 195

Tool #3: Morning Gratitude
Ritual .......................................... 196

Tool #4: Evening Thank-You
Box .............................................. 196

Tool #5: Healthy Evening
Habits .......................................... 197

FOR YOUR KIDS ................. 200

Tool #1: Morning Gratitude
at Breakfast .............................. 201

Tool #2: Three Simple
Morning Stretches .................. 201

Tool #3: Mini Morning
Story ........................................... 204

Tool #4: Short Morning
Meditation ................................ 205

Tool #5: Evening: Thorn,
Bud, Rose .................................. 206

Tool #6: Evening
Thankful Box ............................ 207

NOTES .................................................................... 210

ACKNOWLEDGMENTS ............................................. 213

ABOUT THE AUTHOR ............................................. 215

# INTRODUCTION

Is your household calm?

If you're a parent, the answer is probably a big fat NO. Maybe you're in the throes of chasing after a toddler. Maybe you have angelic children who never get upset and you think you have this parenting thing all figured out. (Ha!) Maybe you count down the hours until bedtime so you can have a glass of wine and cuddle up on the couch in front of Netflix. Maybe you are dealing with teenage drama and dream of your children turning eighteen, moving out, and allowing you to live your best life.

Chances are you've become reactive to your children's behavior. In 2020 especially, we all heard reports of stress, anxiety, and reactive behavior from parents worldwide. Parents felt out of their depth, too wrapped up in juggling home and work life and making ends meet to understand how to deal with their children's pain and fear, much less their own.

» Nearly 50 percent of parents reported significant stress increases due to the lockdown that have negatively impacted their mental and physical health.[1]

» Researchers found that since March 2020, 27 percent of parents reported worsening mental health for themselves, and 14 percent reported worsening behavioral health for their children.[2]

» In 2020, the proportion of children's mental health–related emergency department (ED) visits among all pediatric ED visits for ages 5 to 11 and 12 to 17 years increased approximately 24 percent and 31 percent, respectively.[3]

» 71 percent of parents believe the pandemic took a toll on their child's mental health, and 67 percent of parents wish they'd been more vigilant about their child's mental health from the beginning.[4]

» Even before COVID-19, youth suicide was already at a record high. Suicide is the second leading cause of death among people ages 10 to 24 and has been increasing every year since 2007. The Centers for Disease Control and Prevention reported that suicide was the second leading cause of death among people ages 10 to 34.[5]

The effects of what we've all been through these last few years are real and dire. Instead of just wading through and hoping things get better, it's time for a different approach.

But in our time-crunched society, most of us just don't have the bandwidth to do what it takes, right? We're too busy, too tired, too distracted to figure out what our kids need. And so, we REACT. Despite our best intentions, we are living in a culture where reactive parenting has become the new norm.

We struggle with figuring out how to create a calm household when we live in an unpredictable world. We can't possibly understand how to share the same space with our tiny beloved terrors when we live in a constant state of distraction and reaction. We just aren't sure how to make any of this work.

If your kid's not listening, has seemed to turn into some unrecognizable alien, seems anxious, upset, unruly, or highly reactive, there is something you can do. There is hope!

Wherever you are in your parenting journey, there are always ways to improve, connect, and find calm in the chaos. Instead of repeating the same patterns, feeling overwhelmed or uncertain of what to do next, today is the day you give yourself permission to let go of the guilt and shame around feeling like a "bad" parent or labeling your child in the same way. You and your child are not bad, defective, or wrong. Raising kids is hard, and we all need some good, practical, and effective tools to help us navigate the way.

Reactive parenting comprises the negative behaviors displayed when a parent is frustrated with their child. This often looks like yelling, threatening, screaming, or even hitting. Reactive parenting can also look like over-rewarding or overbribing when the parent is fed up with their child's behavior.

In this book, we will start from a neutral place that addresses both the parent *and* child. Just like in marriage, issues rarely stem from just one party. This book is your toolbox, and the tools inside will help you cultivate a better and calmer home environment for everyone. The first section focuses on the difficulties parents face and tools to address those issues. The second section goes deeper into how to continuously access those tools and help create meaningful change within yourself and your home.

While so many of us reach for parenting books when there's something wrong, this book provides tools that you and your child can tap into together *throughout* the ebb and flow of the child-raising years. It is your family's toolbox for the good days and the not-so-good days. The process all starts with learning first for yourself *and then* teaching your kids.

As a former elementary school teacher, child educator, mental health first aid responder, mindfulness and meditation teacher, and mother of two, I've seen and experienced it all. I've worked with parents at the end of their rope who just wanted to give up on having a good relationship with their children. I've helped parents navigate rocky terrain and implement useful strategies and have seen their households shift seemingly overnight. I've helped a child build confidence when he was overtaken by negative thinking, walked my own daughter through a medical condition that created unbearable anxiety for her, and supported mothers and fathers as they stopped engaging in power struggles and started enjoying their time with their children more.

In this book, I will focus on the most common issues between the parent and child, which range from "My kid's not listening!" to what to do when they hit you; from meltdowns to power struggles; from decreasing screen time to knowing how to navigate parenthood without completely losing your mind in the process. Because none of us are given a manual on *how* to parent, many of us just get swept up in *reactive* parenting instead of taking a *proactive* approach.

These proactive tools help both parent and child explore how to go from practice to action to traction. It's not just about asking how you regulate your kid, but how you regulate yourself. Have you dealt with your own past conditioning and your own shadows? Have you dealt with your own parenting baggage? Have you really taken a look at your own reactions and figured out how you relate to your children and, ultimately, yourself?

I ask because you're not just working on getting your kids to listen; you're also stopping the age-old generational conditioning that's been passed down from your parents, grandparents, and society at large.

At the end of the day, if we continue to normalize our abnormal behavior and keep ourselves in an unregulated state without real tools, then all we're really doing is bouncing between chaotic moments. All we're really doing is *reacting* to our children instead of interacting. It's time to create a new baseline—both for ourselves and our children.

It's time to take a collective, mindful approach to this journey we call parenthood.

At the end of the day, you don't have to parent in a vacuum or meet every stage with resistance and dread. When you show up for yourself, you show up for your family in a more actualized, human state. Let's peel back the layers and show our children what it means to be fully human.

It starts with *you*.

# HOW TO USE THIS BOOK

Each chapter in this book will begin with a universal parenting problem. The first part of every chapter will focus on common self-regulation issues all parents face. I will then guide you through finding solutions to the problem with strategies, tips, and tools from experts, teachers, parental educators, and moms to deal, heal, and cultivate a calmer environment. These will empower you to decrease your reactivity.

I will then give you and your child tools to solve the *same* problem. Think of this as a two-for-one book that focuses on parent and child to address the entire family. The second part of every chapter will take the same approach for children through unique stories, fun worksheets, and even journaling exercises that offer a collaborative approach to self-regulation within the paradigm of family.

In this book, we will explore:

» Poor listening skills

» Morning and nighttime routines

» Tantrums

» Behavioral challenges

» Anger (yours and your child's)

» Meltdowns

» Power struggles

» Fear and the worrying mind

» Sibling rivalry

» Navigating parenthood without completely losing your mind

» The impact of negative thinking on the parent-child relationship

» Mindfulness

» Too much screen time

» Self-care

When it comes to the sections for adults, the chapters build upon each other, so I suggest reading them from beginning to end. However, the kids' sections can be read in chunks, and activities can be used as needed over time (or all at once), depending on the age and needs of the child.

If you are raising a child with a partner and find that just one of you is reading the book, don't fret. Specific activities and tools can be copied and done together as you parent, during family meetings, or whenever it fits your needs.

This book is a guide, and I encourage you to keep coming back to it, tweaking the tools as needed to meet your child's age and temperament. You will be amazed at how these teachings can be used for years within your home to create a more harmonious space.

# WHY I WROTE THIS BOOK

*I left my teaching career for this?* I asked, fuming as my three-year-old son whacked me again on the back of my leg. Blood boiling and eyes as sharp as daggers, I bent down to his level and yelled, "No hitting!" Pulling him upstairs for a time-out, it dawned on me that there had to be a better way. In fact, I had recently read an article about sitting with your child when they were angry. Still boiling over with my own rage, I attempted to sit.

*I got this*, I said to myself. *If I could teach 25 six-year-olds, then I can handle a single three-year-*. . .WHACK! Another smack interrupted my thoughts.

I could no longer sit. I couldn't stand any of this one minute longer.

So I yelled. I yelled in that awful mama yell that makes your throat hurt after and your soul ache with guilt and shame once the words have left your mouth and you can't stuff them back in again.

My blue-eyed boy stared back at me with wide, sad eyes.

At that moment, I made a vow to myself and my son: I would never yell again.

I wish I could tell you that was my last yell. (It wasn't.) I have yelled again since that day. . .but not with that same soul-crushing intensity.

"How?" you may ask.

I'll tell you my secret: I created a calm home.

No, I am not an interior designer, professional organizer, or feng shui specialist. I am a parenting educator and I help other moms, dads, and caregivers learn tools to regulate themselves and support their children.

I came about my career in an internally humbling sort of way. You see, ever since I was old enough to be a mother's helper, I looked after kids in my neighborhood, volunteered at the local preschool, worked with special needs children, and ultimately, became an elementary school teacher.

I love working with children, and taking my first babysitting class at the local rec center was one of my happiest moments, along with a trip to Disneyland and my wedding day.

I felt I was destined to be a teacher and, even more so, I was destined to become a mother.

Prior to having my own children, I couldn't understand the hardships and struggles parents faced with their own children. I had such well-behaved students and never once encountered a babysitting meltdown. To be perfectly honest, I felt that my parenting journey would be easier than most others' because I was more skilled than most. (Ha!)

I laugh now at that misguided thinking. I am now convinced that having two of my own children is harder than teaching twenty-five students, skydiving in flip-flops, or navigating through old Egyptian tombs in 120 degrees Fahrenheit (all of which I have done).

Being a parent is hard for so many reasons—sleepless nights (and not just when they are babies); sibling fights; tantrums in the most embarrassing places, like grocery stores and crowded pools; children refusing to listen; regrets from wishing you had done things differently; peer difficulties; and the list goes on.

Parents are fed up, tuckered out, and, after the crazy year of the pandemic, just about ready to pull their hair out.

Over a short period of time, I changed the entire trajectory of my home life. I changed my home life by reading through as many parenting books as I could find (ones rooted in science and empathy), becoming a certified parenting educator, learning to apply my tools from teaching elementary school to my own home, and creating a larger support network around me of parents who shared the same goals of nurturing their children in a nonreactive environment. In discovering and developing effective parenting tools, my family life went from chaos to calm (not angelic like a photoshopped Instagram pic, but real *calm*).

In 2021 alone, I was a guest on more than 850 radio stations, as well as appearing on national TV shows and in various parenting publications. These accolades are not just a tribute to the work that I am doing, but more importantly, an indication of the *need* parents have right now for tools that will bring more peace into their homes.

Now I help parents get what they really, truly want more than anything in the whole world: happy relationships with their children and a home life that reflects that bond.

Just like when I felt called to be a babysitter when I was just old enough to ride my bike to the store alone, my passion today and for the future is to support parents and children so that we can create a calmer and more peaceful space in a world that can feel very chaotic.

# COMMON PARENTING PROBLEMS & SOLUTIONS

# CHAPTER 1

# USING SELF-REGULATION TO REDEFINE THE WAY YOU PARENT

I hadn't slept in days.

My daughter (the once-independent girl who loved playing in her room alone with her toys) wouldn't leave my side for what felt like the billionth day in a row. It was the peak of the world shutting down, and I was exhausted to my innermost core. I begged her to go play in her room by herself, but she refused.

In my head, I fantasized about screaming "Go play by yourself right now!" I felt unheard and was angry with her newfound worry and the defiance that went with it. I wanted to explode, run away, cry, or all of the above.

My big feelings reminded me of when my children were younger. When my son was three and my daughter was one, I struggled with reactive parenting. I frequently heard rumors of the "terrible twos," but quite honestly thought that I had escaped that phase with such ease that it would be smooth sailing until we hit adolescence. The term I hadn't heard about, but quickly learned, was "threenagers."

**Note:** In recent years, parents have been using the term "threenager" to describe their three-year-olds who show the defiance, attitude, and stubbornness that was historically associated with the teenage years.

And, oh boy, let me tell you—threenagers are as tough as people say they are. That year was filled with defiance, outbursts, and tantrums (my son's and mine)! I just couldn't believe I could find myself so frustrated with my son. In those moments, I would *react*. Admittedly, I didn't have the right tools. And so, power struggles were more common than I care to share. I spent many nights crying and feeling like I was doing it *all wrong*. After going though that very difficult stage, I thought I had overcome a lot of my reactive parenting. I felt like I had made it through, learned many tools along the way, and was again ready for smooth sailing for a while.

I was wrong. When my son was seven and my daughter five, I was back to wanting to bang my head on a wall all over again, but this time I was struggling with my daughter.

At five years old, my daughter had started displaying serious signs of anxiety. She woke up one night during the COVID-19 pandemic, screaming in fear, and wasn't able to calm herself down. For the days and months that followed, she became a ball of anxiety.

Due to my work as a parenting educator and mindfulness/meditation teacher, I was able to help her keep many of the fears at bay by building up her emotional toolbox. I would help her through pretend play so she could release her fears, sing songs together to help her overactive mind, and use mindfulness tools such as noticing the sounds in the room or counting slow and deep breaths. Yet, something still wasn't adding up. Why was her anxiety so intense despite being in a regulated home? Did she need more stability? Was her anxiety coming from the pandemic? Was there a physiological component that I was missing?

After much research and talking to many healthcare professionals, I stumbled upon a possible culprit: *mold*. We ordered an organic acid test to see if she had mold in her body. The test revealed that she had mold toxicity (aka, *lots* of mold in her little body!).

Mold contains toxic chemicals that, when inhaled, can make certain people very sick. Not everyone will have the same sensitivity to mold that my daughter did, and mold can display itself differently from person to person. For my daughter, the mold made her mind spin with worry, like a hamster running on a wheel.

We went on to test our entire home for mold and found that we had mold *behind almost every piece of sheetrock*! Was it a nightmare?! Yes!

We moved out, cleared the mold from her body (and ours) by ingesting binders,[6] and then my daughter went back to her independent and happy self (at least, most of the time; she is still a kid, after all).

I wish I could tell you that through that experience I had nothing but empathy for her and that I was able to stay regulated despite the sleepless nights, intense fearful screaming, and her inability to engage in the activities she had once loved, all while we were doing a major move and home renovation. But that, my friends, would be a lie.

Before the mold was cleared from my daughter's system, I was pushed to my limits time and time again. I wanted to scream right along with her. My tank was empty, I was on calls with doctors and inspectors, which took up every free moment I had, and I was *still* trying to wrap my head around the worldwide pandemic.

There were bumps in the road and times when I had to go back and apologize for my mean tone or harsh words. In short, my home didn't feel like a Pinterest board or a carefully crafted Instagram post.

Instead, it felt like a big, moldy mess.

And although I didn't feel like my parenting game was high, I was very aware that in all this calamity, there was still a steady undertone of love.

Even on the messiest of days, my daughter received the support she needed. This support wasn't luck. The calm that we had amid the chaos wasn't a fluke. In addition to my background as an elementary school teacher, by this time, I had devoted four solid years of coursework, reading, certifications, and studying to understand reactive parenting and how to embody tools that would bring more harmony to my parenting life. The underpinning of peace that we all experienced in such a painful time was a tribute to the same parenting tools *you* are receiving in this book, and it started with the most important tool of all: self-regulation.

# THE KEYSTONE OF SELF-REGULATION

For the purpose of this book, self-regulation will be defined as the ability to calm yourself down and not react to your child with a yell, threat, or bribe to get them to act the way you think they need to act in the moment.

Self-regulation is the keystone that makes all other tools available. It was the reason why, that day when my daughter wouldn't play independently and I was exhausted emotionally and physically, I was able to take a step back to calm myself down and help her feel safer with her worries (funny enough, as I write this chapter more than a year and a half later, she is playing independently with her stuffed animals on the other side of the room, singing the newest tune she just made up).

My daughter's health crisis is an extreme example, I know. Most of your children will not go through a major difficulty like this. I share it though, because it is a dramatic example of the hope that is possible when we build out our parenting toolbox. It is an example of how we can stop being reactive in our parenting approach. I know that if these tools work in the confusion of endless doctor appointments, my daughter feeling beyond awful, countless sleepless nights that involved my daughter shaking with fear, the inability for me to leave her alone because she was feeling so scared, and missed school days—while also caring for her brother who was confused and worried about his little sister—then these tools can (and do) work in homes far and wide. This, my dear reader, is a powerful toolbox.

This toolbox must start with you. It is only by your learning, relearning, and practicing self-regulation that the rest of the tools can be effective for your children.

So, let's pause for a moment and examine why self-regulation must come first. After all, I don't want you to just take my word for it.

Here are two scenarios. See if you can identify the scenario in which the parent self-regulates and the one in which the parent is reactive.

# SCENARIO #1

Your family and another family you love spending time with make plans to go to the beach. You have just spent the morning packing the picnic baskets, putting the towels and beach bags in the car, and getting your kids into their swimsuits (with sunscreen to boot).

It's time to get in the car. When your youngest child suddenly starts crying, you ask him why he is so upset, to which he sobs, "I don't want to go to the beach!"

Taken aback, you tell him that everyone is going to the beach. His friends will be at the beach, and it is time to go *now*; otherwise, you will be late to meet everyone.

"No!" he screams, then runs inside and hides under his bed.

At this point, you are exhausted from preparing all morning, stunned by the abrupt change in behavior, and beyond annoyed because you know you will officially be late if you don't leave this second.

You march upstairs and tell your son that he needs to get in the car now. He doesn't budge, so you tell him that if he gets in the car, you will buy him an ice cream at the beach.

He still won't move.

Angry, you tell him that if he doesn't get in the car, he won't get to watch a movie later.

With no more tools left and feeling beyond upset, you drag him out from under the bed and yell that he better get himself into the car immediately, all while fuming down the stairs as he sulks his way into the car.

# SCENARIO #2

Just like in Scenario #1, you have spent the morning getting ready to meet family friends at the beach, when your son suddenly announces that he doesn't want to go.

Taken aback, you take a deep breath and silently think of three things you appreciate and love about your child, who is disrupting your plan and bringing up feelings of frustration.

In a calm state, you get down on the ground so you are a little below your son's eye level, and you give him a hug and say that you are sorry to hear he doesn't want to go to the beach.

He melts into your arms with a big burst of tears and tells you that the last time he went to the beach, he got saltwater in his eyes, and he is afraid it will happen again.

"Oh, I hate when saltwater gets in my eyes," you tell him. "That must have felt really icky."

Then you ask your son if he has any ideas on how he might prevent getting water in his eyes this time at the beach. Perhaps he suggests swim goggles or sunglasses. Perhaps this time, he doesn't want to go in the water or just wants to put his feet in instead.

After finding a solution, you comment on how proud you are of your son for sharing his feelings and creating a solution to the problem. You and your family get in the car and head out to the beach.

# REFLECTION

*When you read Scenario #1, what feelings does it bring up in you?*

_____

_____

*Now, imagine that you are the child. How would you have felt?*

_____

_____

*Can you think of a time when a similar situation played out in your home? How did you feel after?*

_____

_____

*When you read Scenario #2, what feelings did it bring up in you?*

_____

_____

*Imagine that you are the child. How would you have felt?*

_____

_____

*Can you think of a time when a similar situation played out in your home? How did you feel after?*

_____

_____

In Scenario #1, the parent does not self-regulate and skips right to the common tools of bribing and punishing (aka *reacting*). These tools often cause initial rebellion, followed by the child feeling unheard and angry.

In Scenario #2, the parent is using their self-regulation tool. The child felt heard by the parent, was able to express their fears, and used critical thinking skills to come up with a solution.

Although both scenarios achieved the same goal—getting the child into the car to go to the beach—the tone and feeling of the two scenarios were very different.

Furthermore, the first scenario created a disconnect between the parent and child. The second scenario built trust and connection, which serves to create and maintain the important parent-child bond.

After reading and reflecting on both of these scenarios, you can see how the ability for the parent to self-regulate was of the utmost importance.

The only reason that the parent was able to use their parenting toolbox in Scenario #2 (getting down below her child's eye level, giving a hug, empathizing with the son's feelings, and finding a solution), was because the parent didn't become *reactive*. The parent took the moment to pause and calm down before connecting with the child.

You will learn all those same parenting tools (and more) as we go along, and you'll find yourself having more interactions that play out like the second scenario when you learn to regulate yourself. (Trust me when I say it's a game changer.)

Do we now agree that self-regulation is one of the most important parenting tools we have? Do you see that if we are not regulating *ourselves,* then we have no chance of helping our children learn the tools they need to grow from their mistakes and navigate their tough behavioral moments?

The idea of self-regulation is simple, but maintaining a regulated state is hard when our children are fighting or not listening, or when things feel like a hot mess.

Self-regulation does require some work on your part, and you will need to be patient and kind to yourself as you practice. Remember, though, when you work on self-regulation as a parent or caregiver, you are working toward the ultimate long-term goal all of us have— raising a child who is kind, good natured, curious, honest, and loving.

One day at a time (or even one minute at a time), I invite you to stop yelling, stop threatening, stop bribing, and stop reacting. Join me on the path to *calmer* parenting. It all starts with self-regulation.

Let's dive into Tool #1.

# TOOL #1: PLAN-TO-PAUSE POSTER

The Plan-to-Pause Poster is more than a pretty parenting tool to hang in your home (although you can make it look quite nice!). To understand the importance of the poster, let us start with a quick and very basic overview of a few parts of the brain. Please note that every day, more research is being done on the functions of the brain.

This overview is to help you understand the big-picture idea, but if you are interested in learning more about the brain, I invite you to check out *The Whole-Brain Child* by Daniel J. Siegel and Tina Payne Bryson (one of my favorite books!).

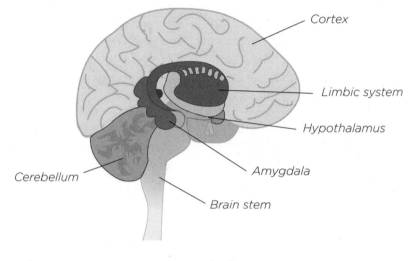

Human brain

**The Cortex:** This outer layer of the brain is home to our prefrontal cortex. Our prefrontal cortex is in charge of executive functions, decision making, and critical thinking (among other things). It is important to note that the prefrontal cortex does not fully develop until a person is around the age of twenty-five.

**The Limbic System:** The two important parts of the limbic area to note for our discussion are the hypothalamus and the almond-shaped amygdala.

When we are stressed, the hypothalamus sends out signals to release stress hormones that can seem protective in the short term, but are harmful over time if our minds continue to perceive many threats (e.g. sibling arguments, back talk, or power struggles).

The other important part of the limbic system is the amygdala, which is associated with our fear response. When we feel threatened, the amygdala can help protect us. This is great when you see your child about to step into the street with a car coming (you will most likely yell "Stop!" and reach out to protect them). It's not helpful if you see your child's behaviors as a threat. The amygdala has direct correlations with the brain stem.

**The Brain Stem:** This part of the brain is often called the "reptilian brain, or lizard brain" because its function is associated with our survival instincts. It is the oldest part of the brain. Clusters of neurons in the brain stem are associated with our fight-flight-or-freeze response. For this, you may want to imagine a lizard in a terrarium that you are closing in on with a stick. The lizard has many survival tools it might employ, one of them being opening its mouth and preparing to fight. When we feel threatened like the lizard, our brain stem gets involved.

Acting from this reptilian part of our brain, we are no longer connected to our prefrontal cortex; thus, we are unable to self-regulate and we become reactive. None of the parenting tools in our parenting toolbox will be very effective when we are in this state of mind.

Because our children don't have a fully developed prefrontal cortex, it is our job to act as theirs. And that means we have to pause long enough to get back into our rational thinking mind (prefrontal cortex) in those moments when we just want to scream. Understanding the way our brain is working in a state of anger and stress can help us work toward a place of regulation.

In the words of Dr. Ian Davis-Tremayne, DC, "Our nervous system is two-third afferent and one-third efferent. . .meaning that we are two-thirds sensory and one-third reactionary. Once we have the right tools in place, we can control our reactions to any situation before the fight-or-flight response takes over. The Plan-to-Pause Poster helps parents not react to their children."

The Plan-to-Pause Poster helps you find tools to go from fight-flight-or-freeze to calm when you are upset!

In my experience, and in the experience of the parents I work with, it is not enough to simply say, "From now on, I am just not going to yell, bribe, or harshly punish." To create a new habit, you must set yourself up for success, and that starts with creating a plan. In the same way you would create a food plan if you went on a diet or an education plan if you wanted to get a degree, this plan will help you be accountable to your new parenting goal of self-regulation.

Ready to dive in and make your poster?

## HOW TO USE THE PLAN-TO-PAUSE POSTER

**1.** Copy the Plan-to-Pause Poster below or download one for free from my website, www.lauralinnknight.com.

**2.** In a calm state, make a list on your poster of five to seven activities for you to do when you are feeling overwhelmed with heavy emotions. You can also add activities and games that you and your child can do together.

**3.** Decorate the poster so it feels meaningful and will be something that you can hang in your home or carry with you. You can take a picture of the poster on your phone and save it in a special album that you can easily find in a frustrating moment. Or, make it the background wallpaper on your phone! You can even laminate a blank poster and use dry erase markers so that you can change the poster anytime you want when new ideas come.

**4.** Don't forget to place the completed poster in an area that will constantly remind you to approach potentially stressful situations in a more relaxed manner and reconnect with your inner calm.

Help keep your cool with the Plan-to-Pause Poster! This poster serves as a reminder to parents that there are funner, calmer alternatives to yelling, bribing, or threatening.

# PLAN TO PAUSE
## FOR PARENTS

Avoid power struggles and yelling matches with your child with the help of the Plan-to-Pause Poster for Parents. All you need to do is add 5 to 7 activities that are quick and easy for you to do in any high-intensity situation to help you remain calm and cool. Make your list with your child and have fun with it! Keep both posters in a place where you and your child will be reminded to pause on a daily basis (e.g., kitchen, bedroom, front door entry, etc.).

For my personal Plan-to-Pause Poster, I have the following listed:

**1.** Go in the other room and take deep breaths.

**2.** Turn on my favorite song.

**3.** Go on a walk around my house or in my backyard.

**4.** Smell a flower, a piece of fruit, or an essential oil.

**5.** Play the game rock, paper, scissors with my child.

**6.** Lay on the floor and put a stuffed animal on my belly. Watch the stuffed animal go up and down with my breath.

Notice that my list contains things that calm me down, as well as an option my child can participate in with me.

I turned to this list all those years ago when my son went into the threenager phase, and it is what I continue to do to this day. My list is so ingrained in me now that most times when I am upset, I am able to pause rather than react (a huge parenting win!).

Don't wait until the next time you are about to lose your temper. Create a plan to pause ahead of time so that you can have a better opportunity to self-regulate!

# TOOL #2: FAVORITE CALMING QUOTES

Keep a running list of your favorite calming quotes. Have you heard the saying, "Neurons that fire together wire together?"

What this means is the more you run a neural circuit in your brain, the more ingrained it becomes. So, for example, if you think negative thoughts day after day, then your mind will tend to drift to the negative when a problem arises. As a way to stop the negative thoughts you have when you are upset with your children, this tool offers positive combat through quotes.

Quotes are plastered all over bumper stickers, magnets, rocks, and cards for a reason. Quotes can lift our mood in tough moments and remind us what our overarching values are. In my weekly Calming

Newsletter, I provide parents with three new quotes each week as a way to build in a natural pause and uplift the mind.

Here's a list of my top ten favorite quotes. I hope they will inspire you to collect more of your own to add to the list.

**1.** "Be happy in the moment, that's enough. Each moment is all we need, not more." —Mother Teresa

**2.** "The greatest communication is usually how we are rather than what we say." —Joseph Goldstein

**3.** "You are the sky. Everything else—it's just the weather." —Pema Chödrön

**4.** "Every individual has a unique contribution." —Jack Kornfield

**5.** "Observe the space between your thoughts, then observe the observer." —Hamilton Boudreaux

**6.** "Few of us ever live in the present. We are forever anticipating what is to come or remembering what has gone." —Louis L'Amour

**7.** "Let go of your mind and then be mindful. Close your ears and listen!" —Rumi

**8.** "With mindfulness, you can establish yourself in the present in order to touch the wonders of life that are available in that moment." —Thich Nhat Hanh

**9.** "Try to be a rainbow in someone else's cloud." —Maya Angelou

**10.** "A good laugh is sunshine in the house." —William Makepeace Thackeray

# TOOL #3: DAILY WRITING REFLECTIONS

Much of our ability to self-regulate will reflect our internal state. Daily journaling and writing exercises can help us maintain a more grounded place of peace.

I invite you to explore what feels best for you in this process. One approach would be to freewrite whatever comes to mind in a journal each day, then finish up with one of the prompts below.

Another suggestion would be to respond to one prompt each day, or you could answer all the prompts each day.

This exercise might feel like a *have to* in the beginning, but over time it will transform into a *get to*.

Your well-being and your relationship with your children are in your hands. I hope you will embrace all the goodness that comes from these tools!

# DAILY PROMPTS

**1.** *Write three things you appreciate about your child/children today.*

_____

_____

_____

**2.** *What is one thing you did well today?*

_____

_____

**3**. *What was one act of kindness you practiced today (either toward yourself or someone else)?*

_____

_____

**4.** *What is going well in your life?*

_____

_____

**5.** *What is one thing that made you smile today?*

_____

_____

# TOOL #4: THE DOS AND DON'TS OF SELF-REGULATION

Congratulations, you have just engaged three tools to help you access one of the most important parenting tools we can have in our parenting toolbox!

As mentioned before, self-regulation is simple in theory, but can be very difficult to access in those super-frustrating moments: Cheerios on the ground, a sister hitting her brother, paint on the wall, Legos down the toilet, being told by your child that they hate you, or the classic door-slamming fight—all these make you want to just pull your hair out, right?

Here are the dos and don'ts around self-regulation to set yourself up for success and remind you to keep practicing your tools. You've got this!

## DOS AND DON'TS OF SELF-REGULATION

| Dos | Don'ts |
|---|---|
| » Have a plan to pause. | » Expect that you will always be able to self-regulate (this is a process). |
| » Write your plan down. | |
| » Keep a copy of your plan in your house, in your car, and on your phone. | » Give up on trying your best each day. |
| » Be patient with yourself, and when you lose it, circle back with your child and apologize. | » Shame, blame, or guilt yourself if you yell or have a reactive parenting moment: this spiral will only make self-regulation harder. |
| » Keep remembering the science of the brain to help you understand your anger better and calm down more easily. | » Blame your kids in those frustrating parenting moments (remember that they are learning just like you, and all kids inherently want to be good. When they misbehave there is often something deeper going on—more of that to come later). |
| » Keep calm cards handy for those upsetting moments (you will find these in Chapter 2). | |
| » Keep creating a calmer state by reading positive quotes and responding to daily journal prompts. | |

# FOR YOUR KIDS

Now that you are practicing self-regulation as a parent, let's look at how your child can learn this important tool as well. After all, this book is all about the family coin, and we must look at both sides to create the balance and peacefulness that we all so very much crave. When your child learns the tool of self-regulation alongside you, you will quickly find that the number of reactions from you and your child decrease, as you and your child are working together more cohesively.

The kids' sections of each chapter are designed for you to read aloud to your child. They are written with children ages four to ten in mind (although you know your child best and can choose what activities feel most effective given your child's personality and temperament). Keep in mind that there are many tools in each section, so you may want to share the tools over a period of time.

As you go through the kids' sections, be patient if your child doesn't gravitate to each tool right away.

In my many years of working with children, I have observed that some children are slow to adapt to new tools, while others want to try them all at once, and others seem like they are disinterested only to one day surprise you by using several tools they've retained but haven't articulated.

My point: keep teaching the tools. Remember your long-range goals of creating a calmer home and teaching your child tools that will help them grow and maintain their kind, good-natured, curious, honest, and loving selves.

The rest of this chapter will now be written for you to read to your child.

**Dear Friends,**

My name is Laura, and I am a teacher. I have two kids of my own, Oliver and Grace. I wrote this book for kids just like you.

Here are some cool tools you can use whenever you feel mad.

All kids feel angry sometimes (just like grown-ups). When you feel angry, you may notice that you often feel the mad inside your body.

For some kids, it feels hot in their hands, and they want to hit. Other kids feel their heart pounding and they want to yell. Other kids want to run away and hide.

In fact, being angry is so common that it would be helpful for us to take a moment and think of a time you felt angry recently.

Close your eyes or stare softly at the ground. Think of a time when you were *really angry* about something.

What were you angry about?

What did you do when you were angry?

Did you feel the anger anywhere in your body?

If you remember where you felt the mad in your body, you can color a picture of it in the outline on page 28. Pretend the mad is a color or several colors, and show where you felt the mad in your body.

If you don't remember where you felt the mad, you can take a guess or come back and color this page the next time you get upset.

Does your anger always have a certain color or colors, or does it change?

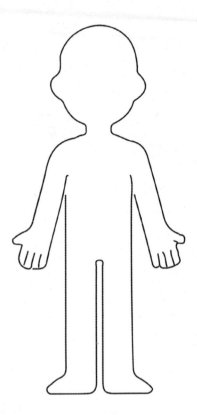

If you would like to, show your picture to your grown-up and tell them about what you drew.

That feeling of mad is a feeling that everyone in the whole world has. Here's something important to remember. Are you ready?

It is totally okay to be mad.

Even though everyone gets mad, and that feeling makes us want to yell, run away, or even hurt someone else, there are better choices that you can make. It is never okay to hurt someone else or yourself.

This book was written to help you make better choices by teaching you tools you can use throughout each day. One way to make better choices is to learn new tools for calming down when you are upset.

Let's imagine that you are building a toolbox. Usually a toolbox has a hammer, a screwdriver, nails, a wrench, maybe a saw, and any other tools that can be used to fix and build things.

**BREAK FREE FROM REACTIVE PARENTING**

Think of this book as your problem-solving toolbox for when you have big feelings or troubles that you need help working out.

So, let's start building your problem-solving toolbox right now with tools for when you get mad.

# TOOL #1: PLAN-TO-PAUSE POSTER

Sometimes, when you are really upset, it is hard to control your body and your words. This is true for you and for your grown-ups. Staying calm isn't always easy. But you can learn to avoid getting so mad. That starts with making a plan.

By deciding ahead of time what you can do the next time you get upset, you are more likely to stay calm when your big, angry feelings take over.

Make this poster with your grown-up and hang it up in your house to remember your plan.

Here is how you can make the poster:

**1.** Ask your grown-up to copy the Plan-to-Pause Poster below or download one for free from my website, www.lauralinnknight.com.

**2.** Think of five to seven things you can do when you are feeling angry and write them on your poster.

**3.** Decorate the poster and hang it in a place that will remind you to use your tools the next time you are mad. If you can't read yet, draw pictures so you will remember what you wrote, or have your grown-up take pictures of you pretending to do each thing on your list and glue those on your poster.

# PLAN TO PAUSE
## FOR KIDS

Kids, here's your own Plan-to-Pause Poster! List your top 5 to 7 favorite things to do that make you happy and feel calmer. Work with your grown-up to come up with your list. You can color, decorate, and draw on your poster and make it extra special—this poster is yours, after all!

**BREAK FREE from REACTIVE PARENTING**

Here is an example of the list my daughter made for her Plan-to-Pause Poster:

**1.** Ask mom or dad for help.

**2.** Color a picture.

**3.** Play with stuffed animals.

**4.** Lie down with a stuffed animal and snuggle.

**5.** Ask for a hug.

**6.** Make a special place in the house where I can calm down.

Remember that you are just beginning to learn these are tools. It took a long time to learn to ride a bike (or maybe you are still practicing)? And it can take the same amount of practice with this tool. Be patient and kind to yourself as you learn. If you forget to use your tools the next time you are mad, you can always always, *always* try again!

# TOOL #2: BIG BELLY BREATHS

Did you know that scientists have studied taking big belly breaths? This type of deep breathing is proven to calm your body and help you feel better.

Think of your body as a car, racing around and burning lots of gas. Taking deep belly breaths slows and steadies your body like the brakes in a car.

Let's try it together!

Find a comfortable place to sit or lie down.

If you are sitting, I suggest sitting straight in a chair, or you can sit tall on the ground with your back straight and your knees "criss-cross applesauce" (also known as cross-legged).

Take a deep breath in through your nose and into your belly. Place your hand on your belly and feel as it rises with air.

Let the breath out through your mouth.

Again, take a deep breath in through your nose and into your belly.

Let the breath out through your mouth.

Try at least five or six deep breaths and see how you feel afterward.

# TOOL #3: SEVEN WONDERFUL PICTURE BOOKS TO READ

Do you like reading books? I do! Sometimes reading a book about someone who has the same feelings we do can really help. Here is a list of books about feeling mad or disappointed that you and your grown-up can look for at the bookstore or library. See how you feel after reading them and ask your grown-up any questions you have after; or, if they spark any more ideas for staying cool and calm when you are upset, talk about them.

**1.** *Last Stop on Market Street* by Matt de la Peña

**2.** *When Miles Got Mad* by Sam Kurtzman-Counter and Abbie Schiller

**3.** *When Sophie Gets Angry—Really, Really Angry* by Molly Bang

**4.** *Moody Cow Meditates* by Kerry Lee MacLean

**5.** *Grumpy Bird* by Jeremy Tankard

**6.** *Peaceful Piggy Meditation* by Kerry Lee Maclean

**7.** *Grumpy Monkey* by Suzanne Lang

# TOOL #4: WHEN YOU'RE MAD—BREATHE WITH THE BIG BAD WOLF

Have you heard the story of the *Three Little Pigs*? If you have, you remember that the Big Bad Wolf got so mad that he used his *huff* and *puff* to blow down a house made of straw, a house made of sticks, and he almost blew down a house made of bricks. If you haven't heard the story, ask your grown-up to read it or tell it to you!

I love that story so much that I made up a new activity for children because, after years of *huffing* and *puffing* and blowing down houses, I was sure the Big Bad Wolf was tired of being a bad guy (after all, working as a villain is a very lonely business). I wanted him to learn to do something good with his strong *huffs* and *puffs*, so I changed his name (just call him Wolf) and his menacing ways. Now, instead of *huffing* and *puffing* and blowing things down, he. . .

*huff*s and *puff*s and. . .

spreads calm all around!

Here is how he uses his *huff* and *puff* to calm down (just like you did with your Big Belly Breaths)!

Stand up tall and look at yourself in the mirror.

Wolf loves the way that his *huff* sounds like the swoosh of the wind.

And his *puff* sounds like the whoosh of a breeze.

*With your back straight,*

*Take a deep huff in. Let your belly fill with air.*

*Take a big puff out. Blow the air awwaaayyy.*

Try doing this at least six times! This is a great tool to use when you are mad, and Wolf uses it all the time to help himself calm down!

I bet you are getting really good with your tools by now and building a super-cool toolbox! Bravo!

I have one more tool to share with you in this chapter: coloring pages!

# TOOL #5: COLORING PAGES TO HELP CHILL OUT

Sometimes all we need is a break to start feeling better.

Grab a glass of water and a snack. Go find some paper, a box of crayons or colored pencils, and a cozy place to sit.

Notice the way the colors look as you put them on the page. Be aware of the way the pencil or crayon feels in your hand and invite your body and mind to relax!

You should be proud of all the new tools you are learning.


With love,

Laura

# CHAPTER 2

# WHO HAS THE POWER?

"It's time to brush your teeth!" I said.

I hurriedly shoved everything into my bag and searched for my keys. I waited to hear the running water and the steady tap of the toothbrush being dried. Instead. . .nothing.

With another precious minute gone, I tried again: "Go brush your teeth."

Instead of complying and feeling my sense of urgency to get out the door *right this minute*, my kids were casually playing with toys in the living room.

I stood at the edge of the door, annoyance steadily pushing in. "Kids, go brush your teeth right this second or no shows later."

My kids still didn't budge.

I was floored. *Didn't they care about shows? Why were they not listening to me?* All of my patience flying out the window, I tried again. "Either brush your teeth right now, or you're having a big consequence."

"Ugh, fine!" they slammed their toys down, stomped into the bathroom, and brushed their teeth for approximately 3.5 seconds. We now had approximately three minutes to get out the door, and jackets and shoes were nowhere in sight.

"We have to go now. Where are your shoes?"

"I don't know," they both said.

Cue full-blown R-A-G-E.

You get the scene here, right? You are now officially engaged in a power struggle.

# WHAT IS A POWER STRUGGLE?

A power struggle is when a child refuses to do something and you, as the parent, are insisting that it needs to be done *right this second or else*. This ongoing back and forth causes a "struggle" because both you and your child want complete control of the situation.

In the example above, it can be helpful to remember what we learned about the brain in Chapter 1. At this point of frustration, both you and your child are operating from that reptilian part of the brain. And both of you are most likely feeling angry, defensive, and ready to attack.

Power struggles show up in most homes around the common topics of getting ready in the morning in a timely manner to leave the house, potty training for younger tots, mealtimes and food frustrations, cleaning up toys and rooms, chores, screen time, and bedtime routines (including the infamous brushing of the teeth).

Power struggles can also present in other ways, of course. I remember when my daughter was three, she abruptly stopped wanting to walk down the stairs in our house alone and insisted that I hold her hand. Of course, it wasn't always possible for me to walk her down the stairs. That left me feeling frustrated, at odds with her demand. It was the perfect opportunity for a power struggle to take place.

The important point to remember in any power struggle, though, is that it takes two to participate. There cannot be a power struggle if you don't engage in it.

The question then becomes, "How do you gracefully navigate these moments?" After all, we need our children to be able to get dressed in the morning, learn to use the bathroom, eat healthy food, clean up their rooms, brush their teeth and, in my case, walk down the stairs without always holding my hand.

If you are the parent of an older child, you have gone through many of these hard topics and gotten to the other side of most of them.

Most likely, you survived potty training and your child can now use the bathroom (yay!). You remember the days of your child refusing to get buckled into their car seat, and it is no longer such a fight. It is helpful to have this experience, because you can trust that in time, these "problems" will sort themselves out. My daughter hasn't asked me to walk her down the stairs in years!

With that said, many of you may also be looking back on those experiences and wondering if it had to feel so dang hard in the moment. Did you *have* to fight over the car seat that many times? Could you have navigated mealtimes a little more easily? Can you successfully avoid future power struggles that arise?

Yes, power struggles do not have to happen as often. Yes, we can lovingly detach from many power struggles by using our newfound toolbox.

And, luckily, after reading this chapter, you will no longer have to fall prey to the power struggle, because these tools will help you stay out of your reptilian brain and move back into the rational thinking part of your brain (Hip, hip, hooray!).

# TOOL #1: MORNING ROUTINE

Let us start by looking at a typical power struggle taking place in homes around the world today: the morning routine.

Mornings with a child can be stressful. Getting your child fed, brushed (*teeth and hair!*), dressed, and out the door in a timely manner can leave you feeling frustrated and overwhelmed, all before 8 a.m.

Creating a morning routine can help get everyone out the door more smoothly and, thus, decrease your stress. Furthermore, creating a morning routine will offer many wonderful opportunities beyond just leaving the house in a more peaceful way—morning routines will help your child learn time-management skills, cooperation, and how to follow through with a plan.

As a family, you will experience smoother transitions, less nagging, and a more peaceful home environment to start the day. The best part about creating a morning routine is that it can be simple and fun!

# MORNING ROUTINE POSTER

In my experience, the best way to establish a morning routine is to *create the routine together with your child*. It is important that you do not skip this very important step.

When you create a routine without a child, the routine becomes more authoritarian, and power struggles often arise. Instead, I suggest finding a quiet moment to sit down with your child and ask:

*"How do we get ready in the morning?"*

Most children respond by listing a few things they do each morning: get dressed, eat breakfast, and brush teeth. You can help curate the list by adding things they may have missed. In this example, you could add brushing hair, getting backpacks ready, and putting on shoes.

Now comes the fun part for your child! Get out paper, markers, stickers, and tape. Be creative while you help your child make their very own morning routine poster to be hung up in the house.

When my children were little and couldn't yet draw, I took photos or drew pictures of them doing each activity on their list, and we glued them on poster board so they could visually see each step of the morning routine.

Today, my nine-year-old can draw the posters, and my seven-year-old can decorate hers with stickers and glitter glue.

Because the routine is created with your child as a *collaborative* process, it becomes the guiding reminder in the morning. Your child will want to participate in following the steps on the poster because they created it!

Of course, there will still be messy mornings when a child doesn't want to brush their teeth, but you will be amazed by how much easier getting out the door becomes as you help your child learn to follow the steps outlined on their poster.

When you are first starting your morning routine, keep the list simple and easy to understand.

As I mentioned before (but it bears repeating), for a younger child who can't yet read, be sure to include visuals such as pictures or drawings so they can understand their poster. Let your child's creativity shine as they make a routine poster they feel proud to hang up.

## MORNING ROUTINE DOS AND DON'TS

| Dos | Don'ts |
|---|---|
| » Keep your poster easy to follow.<br><br>» Make things as clear as possible for the routine to be accomplished (you might include picking out clothes the night before, putting shoes by the front door, and having a hairbrush ready in your child's bedroom).<br><br>» Guide your child back to the routine poster when they get distracted. This can be as simple as asking, "What's the next step on your poster?" | » Engage in power struggles. Instead, simply keep going back to the poster and ask your child, "What needs to happen next?"<br><br>» Worry if it takes some time for your child to learn the routine. Trust that your child is learning a new skill and you are teaching tools that will last a lifetime.<br><br>» Use the morning routine poster as a way to bribe or punish. You are teaching your child to develop time management and life skills, so be gentle with yourself and your child. |

If you enjoy making a morning routine poster with your child, you can use this same strategy to create a bedtime routine!

I remember the days when getting out the door felt like a battle and a rush. Those mornings are far and few between in my home after taking the time to teach my children these habits and inviting them to create the routines with me.

The beauty of highlighting solutions to the morning routine power struggle is it gives us a chance to pick out the tools that support many other power struggles as well.

Below are the tools I offered as morning routine solutions (and a few bonus tools) that will also help you navigate the trickiest of power struggles.

# TOOL #2: CALMING CARDS

Going back to our very important tool of self-regulation, we must remain calm if we are going to successfully disengage from a power struggle.

Again, it takes two to fight, and it is our job as the parents to remain calm as much as we can (and believe me, I can personally say that is much easier said than done).

The Calming Cards are similar in their intention as the Plan-to-Pause Poster. However, instead of having you come up with your own list of calming activities, the cards include calming tools that I have seen work very effectively for parents. You may find that some of these tools are similar to what you put on your poster (that is great!), or you may discover some new tools for your toolbox.

Regardless of if these tools are old or new, I encourage you to keep a copy of them on hand. You may think as you are reading this book that you will retain the tools. However, we know that when your lizard brain gets activated, it will be harder to get back into your prefrontal cortex and make rational choices. These cards are your loving reminder to get back into the rational thinking part of your mind.

If you are stressed and feel like you have zero control of your child's temper tantrum, know that these Calming Cards were designed to help *you* take a moment to calm overwhelming emotions and thoughts with simple, positive practices. Rather than reacting to your child's moods and meltdowns, you can pull out one (or more) of the Calming Cards and do the short exercise. Then, you can return to the situation with a calmer, more rational mindset and resolve the problem with smiles, not stress!

Pages 41–42 show what the cards look like. You can download a free copy from www.LauraLinnKnight.com/freebies, or take pictures and keep the Calming Cards in an album on your phone so you always have them nearby.

### GET MOVING

Short bursts of exercises can dramatically change your current mental state and give you a moment to pause and recollect yourself.

Do 10 jumping jacks or pushups, run around the backyard, stretch, or do anything that will help you get out of the reactive mindset.

Invite your child to join you and do some child-friendly exercises to help lighten the mood and break the tension!

### BRING OUT YOUR INNER ARTIST

Take a moment to redirect your attention by drawing, coloring, painting, or journaling.

Have a blank notebook or sketchbook and other tools to help you relax with a more creative approach.

Ask your child to join you with their own coloring books and bond over some artistic fun!

### DO A 10-SECOND COUNTDOWN

Diffuse any bubbling emotion by counting to 10 while breathing deeply.

### HELPFUL QUOTES

There is a reason quotes are plastered all over bumper stickers, magnets, rocks, and cards. Quotes can lift your mood in tough moments and remind you what your overarching values are. Here are 3 of my favorite quotes. If you find they help, start a list of more of your favorites!

"Do the best you can until you know better. Then when you know better, do better."
- Maya Angelou

"A few simple tips for life: feet on the ground, head to the skies, heart open...quiet mind."
- Rasheed Ogunlaru

'That's life: starting over, one breath at a time."
- Sharon Salzberg

### TAKE A BREAK

Before you react or respond to your child's temper tantrum or meltdown, pause and breathe.

If you can, remove yourself from the situation momentarily to focus on your inner calm. You can go to the bathroom and run cold water over your hands or sit down somewhere and take a few calming breaths.

You can also create a mental or written list of the top 3-5 activities you can do when you need a break. Memorize the list and repeat the actions to yourself so that you can remember to do one or more next time.

Calming Cards for grown-ups

## GRATITUDE LIST

Pause and make a written or mental list of three things about your child that you are grateful for!

Sometimes, you can get caught up in a moment of frustration with your child. Before you react, pause and make a written or mental list that focuses on what you love and are grateful for about your child.

## TAKE DEEP BREATHS

Scientists have studied the effects of the breath on the body. Deep breathing calms your body and makes you feel better.

Think of your body as a car, racing around and burning lots of ghas. Deep breathing slows and steadies your body like brakes in a car. This deep breathing signals the parasympathetic nervous system, which controls our rest state.

When you're feeling stressed out or feel a reaction coming up, take a few deep breaths ... re you respond to your child.

## PLAY YOUR FAVORITE SONG

Put on your favorite upbeat song that gets you in a lighter mood and have a little dance party!

Move your body, sing along with your favorite tunes, and enjoy the few minutes alone before you respond to your child.

## REMEMBER YOUR BRAIN

Did you know that the prefrontal cortex of your brain is in charge of rational decision making while the lower part of your brain—the amygdala—is responsible for fight, flight, and freeze, aka your reactions?

Knowing the science behind the brain ca help you fully understand yourself and your child and make it easier for you to stay calm when you feel like you're losing your cool. When you and your child are upset, you are both using the lower part of your brain to respond to the situation.

However, your child will not fully develop their prefrontal cortex until they are 25, so it's up to you to act as their prefrontal cortex.

## TALK TO YOURSELF

Self-talk is important, and calling yourself a bad parent or a parent that doesn't know anything won't help with bringing peace in your inner world or outside.

Watch the way you talk to yourself and use positive affirmations such as

"I'm okay."

"I'm calm."

"I'm relaxed."

"I can do this without yelling."

Calming Cards for grown-ups

**BREAK FREE FROM REACTIVE PARENTING**

# TOOL #3: THE 3 P'S: PROBLEM-SOLVE, PLAN, PATIENCE

I was in the midst of a power struggle with my kids. My son was annoying his sister at the public pool, and she was jumping on him in retaliation. I asked them both nicely to please stop. Nothing. I tried to redirect them, and I even tried to change the mood with some other swimming suggestions. None of my tools were working. The kids' argument had now become my argument (sigh!).

In that moment of the power struggle, trying to practice the 3 P's would have been pointless. My kids were too upset and I was too irritated.

I told them firmly that I needed them to get out of the pool and sit on the chairs nearby. I was kind, but very clear with a specific boundary.

There are times when children will be so upset that they will not yet be ready for the tools in this book. Sometimes the tools can help stop the cycle and get them back into good spirits (the Calming Cards for kids are great for this), but other times, they need you to set a clear limit.

Based on the research I have done around what is most beneficial for a child's well-being, I don't use punishment methods such as long timeouts, I never spank, and if there is a consequence, I try to have it relate to the situation at hand (this is called a logical or natural consequence).

For this example, getting out of the pool to sit for a few minutes made much more logical sense than taking away a toy or threatening no television when we got home.

After my son and daughter sat for a few minutes with me nearby, I could see that they were calm enough to engage in conversation.

I began with the first P: problem-solve.

I approached my son first: "Hey honey, I noticed you were getting really upset with your sister in the pool. What's going on?"

Be aware that I am not making assumptions or reprimanding my son for his behavior. Instead, I am curious so that I can get feedback from him and understand his feelings.

In this case, he was upset because his sister was jumping on him, and he didn't want to play in that way.

"Oh, I know how frustrating that can be," I said to him. "I wonder what we could do so it feels fair for both of you."

My son thought that playing separately from his sister in the pool for a while would work as a solution.

This is how the conversation went with my daughter:

"Hey sweetie, I noticed that you and your brother were getting upset in the pool. What was going on for you?"

In her case, she didn't like that when she jumped on him, he jumped back on her.

Her solution? To keep their hands to themselves.

Because they both had very similar solutions, we dove straight into the second P: plan.

Our plan, in this case, was simple. Both kids wanted to take space and keep hands to themselves in the pool for a while.

Sometimes, creating a plan will require more negotiation and compromise on everyone's part. That is perfectly normal and okay. This is an opportunity for your children to use their critical-thinking tools and build their problem-solving muscles. You can help your child find a solution that feels good for them and for you.

It was now time for the last P: patience.

If you have ever decided that you would start to work out daily, only to discover that on day three, you suddenly forgot about your resolve and the gym seemed like a long-ago dream, then you can understand that just because your child has found a solution to their problem, it may not automatically stick (some plans are easier said than done).

This is where the third P of patience comes in.

Did my kids take space from jumping on each other in the pool? Yes! Did they take that space for the short amount of swim time that was left at the pool? No! They needed more reminders, but going back to the plan they had agreed upon and created made their willingness to listen and respect the agreement that much greater.

Kids are so often told what to do without getting the opportunity to problem-solve. Asking them to actively participate in what needs to be done can dramatically shift the tone and mood of the situation.

# TOOL #4: ORDER LESS AND ASK MORE

This leads us right into the third tool for avoiding power struggles—giving fewer orders and being more curious.

Many of you may know a classic book called, *No, David!* by David Shannon.

In this hilarious picture book, David is getting into all sorts of mischief, with his mother telling him "No!" on every page.

When I read this book, I can't help but think about all the times our children are being told "No!" They hear it at school, at after-school activities, and especially, at home.

It's no wonder that kids get upset when we order them to brush their teeth, hurry up and find their coats, stop whining, be quiet, and then add sprinkles of *No! No! No!* to all those orders. Honestly, how would you feel if you were in their shoes?

An easy fix for this is to *order less and ask more*. This is a simple tool that has been very helpful for the parents I've worked with over the years and was an especially effective tool for me in the classroom.

Order less and ask more could sound like this:

» Put on your pajamas = *What do you need to do to get ready for bed?*

» Hurry up and find your shoes = *Do you know where your shoes might be?*

» Stop whining = *How can you talk so I can understand you better?*

» Be quiet = *How can you talk in a voice that is soft like a mouse?*

How do you feel when you hear the ordering statement vs. the asking statement?

How do you think your kids will feel if you ask more and order less?

This tool is highlighted in the morning routine poster and can be used very effectively around bedtime.

Parents have avoided many power struggles simply by changing their approach and tone to the everyday things that need to get done. Furthermore, when parents change their approach to how they communicate with their child and have consistent routines in place, reactive parenting significantly diminishes. I have seen this countless times with children and parents I have worked with and in my own home as well.

I will share more about this particular tool and what other educators in the parenting field have to say about it in Chapter 7.

# TOOL #5: EMPATHY THROUGH STORYTELLING

The last tool in our power struggle toolbox is empathy through storytelling.

**Empathy (noun):** *the ability to understand and share the feelings of another.*[7]

Empathy for our children can make a world of difference when it comes to diffusing power struggles. Imagine you went to your friend and told them how hurt you were because you weren't invited to another friend's birthday celebration. Imagine that when you confided this hurt to your friend, they responded by telling you to stop complaining and get over it. Would you feel better? Would you go to that friend for support again?

Our children's feelings can seem so silly sometimes, and the intensity of them can overwhelm us. But their feelings are real to them, and it is important for us to acknowledge rather than ignore the feelings or tell our kids to get over it.

As Dr. Daniel J. Siegel writes in *The Whole-Brain Child*, "It's also crucial to keep in mind that no matter how nonsensical and frustrating our child's feelings may seem to us, they are real and important to our child. It's vital that we treat them as such in our response."

When a child doesn't want to eat a meal, get in the car, or get dressed in the morning, take a moment to empathize with their feelings. Tell them you understand and hear their frustration and sadness.

Then, go a step beyond that initial empathy and tell them about a time you felt the same frustration or sadness.

I remember hating it as a child when my mom would brush my hair. I often didn't want to go to bed because I was scared of the dark. Eating meals sometimes felt like torture (especially when it was tofu and vegetables for what felt like the millionth time).

I share those stories with my children because doing so helps them understand that they are not alone. It is possible to hold a clear limit while still helping your child feel heard, seen, and understood.

Empathy through stories can bypass many power struggles in your home and create a closer bond between you and your child.

As we conclude the section for you about power struggles, I invite you to use the journal prompts on the following page to reflect on how you navigate power struggles over the next several weeks with your new set of tools. Please remember to practice self-compassion as you learn new ways of interacting with your children. This is an opportunity to create habits that will last a lifetime, but it starts one minute at a time and it might be rocky at first.

# POWER STRUGGLE JOURNAL

Date: _____

*What power struggle(s) came up today?*

_____

_____

*What tools did you use?*

_____

_____

*What went well?*

_____

_____

*What would you change?*

_____

_____

*Bonus: List two things that you are grateful for about each member of your family.*

_____

_____

The next section is written directly for you to read aloud to your children. Because it takes two to tango and two to be in a power struggle, this section will help your child understand what is going on in a power struggle and empower them with tools.

# FOR YOUR KIDS

**Dear Friends,**

You know how grown-ups ask you to do things, like get ready for bed, put away your toys, eat your dinner, or take a shower?

Sometimes you are happy to listen to your grown-ups without any arguments at all, right?

Other times, though, you might be right in the middle of a game that you don't want to stop, or you feel too tired to clean up, or maybe you had a hard day and now your body and mind feel grumpy.

When you feel grumpy with your grown-ups and don't want to listen, sometimes an argument might start.

To help you understand what is going on in this situation, we can look at two parts of your brain.

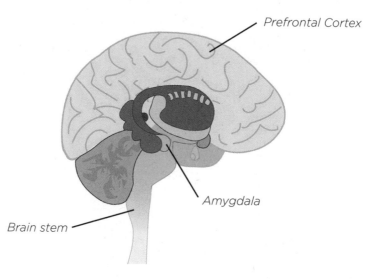

Human brain

The upper part of your brain is home to your prefrontal cortex. This is a wise part of the mind, and it can help you calm down when you are having big feelings.

In the lower part of your brain, you have what we call the amygdala and the brain stem. This area of your brain is active when you are angry, want to run away, or get super scared.

The tools in the cool problem-solving toolbox that you are learning about will help you stay in that upper part of your brain—the wise part.

It isn't always easy to stay calm when you are having big feelings and frustrations. Just like we talked about ways to stay calm in Chapter 1, the tools here can help you when you are frustrated. These tools can help you stay away from arguments too!

# TOOL #1: KIDS CALMING CARDS

Remember how you made that really awesome Plan-to-Pause Poster on page 31? You came up with ideas to help calm your body down when you were upset. I have some Calming Cards that you can use just like your Plan-to-Pause Poster. Ask your grown-up to download them from www.LauraLinnKnight.com/freebies. These Calming Cards may have a few extra-fun ideas you might not have thought of yet (and they are tools that my kids love to use too).

You can try them with your grown-up now!

**CLAP WITH ME**

A sailor went to sea, sea, sea, to see what she could see, see, see, but all that she could see, see, see, was the bottom of the deep blue sea, sea, sea.

We are joyful.

**I'LL TRACE YOUR HANDS**

I'll trace your hands.

Now you trace mine.

We are loved.

**ROCK, PAPER, SCISSORS**

Let's play rock, paper, scissors!

We can laugh.

**REPEAT AFTER ME**

I'll clap a simple beat for you to repeat.

Now it is your turn!

We are silly.

**HUG TIME**

Would you like a hug?

May I please have a hug?

We care about each other (a lot).

**COUNT EACH STEP**

Let's go for a short walk outside. We can count each step. How many will it take?

We are trying our best.

Calming Cards for kids

**Who Has the Power?**

Calming Cards for kids

# TOOL #2: FLOWER-PETAL TRICK

Just like you get frustrated sometimes, I do too! One of my tricks for feeling better when I am really upset with someone is to think of things that I like about them. Sounds wild, right? But it really works!

Let me tell you about a time that I used this trick. My family was traveling in Costa Rica, and my son was being extra goofy at bedtime. Like most moms, I wanted him to get into bed for story time. And, like many young boys, my son couldn't get into bed because he was too busy doing something else—in this case, telling jokes to his little sister. I was tired from all our traveling and was about to get really mad, when I remembered my flower petal trick.

To use the flower-petal trick, you can either imagine a big flower with five petals or get out a piece of paper and draw a big flower.

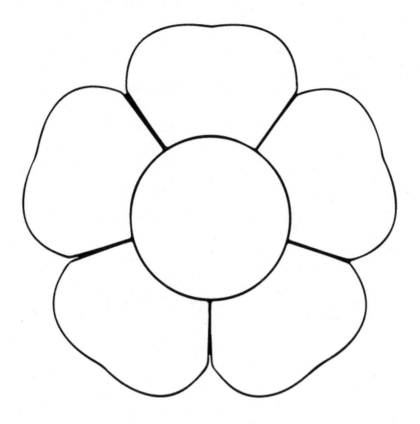

If you imagine the flower in your mind, think of five things you like about the person who is upsetting you. Imagine that each nice thing goes with one of the petals on the flower.

If you draw the flower, you can color in the center of the flower and make it look just the way you want. Then you can write (or draw) one nice thing about the person in each of the five petals.

Let's try this activity now with your grown-up. Take out a piece of paper and some markers. Draw the center of the flower and make five petals going around it. In each petal, write or draw one thing that you love about your parent. Make sure that they make a flower for you as well! After you have both finished your flowers, you can share them with each other. My children have the flowers that I made them in their room!

This action of thinking kind things about another person is a way of finding gratitude.

Gratitude is thinking about what you like about your life, yourself, and your friends. It is being thankful for what you have and being thankful for others.

Did you know you can actually be upset with someone while being grateful for them at the same time? Being in gratitude for the person you feel upset toward helps you feel less angry in the moment and avoid an argument. It also helps your body and mind relax so you can find a solution to the problem.

In the case of my son not wanting to go to bed, after I thought of five things I was grateful for about him and calmed down, we agreed to do a comedy show in the morning (which was spectacular) and stop the jokes for that night so everyone could get some sleep.

You can do a similar activity with your family or friends when you are not upset. It will keep your gratitude growing and help you in the times when you are feeling upset with someone.

This flower petal activity is inspired by the late Zen master Thich Nhat Hanh and his book about mindfulness for children, called *Planting Seeds*.

# TOOL #3: MINI GATHERING

If you notice that you are starting to get into an argument with your grown-up (or even a sibling), you can ask them if you can pause and have a mini gathering.

A mini gathering is a short meeting. It is a chance for you to figure out why everyone is getting so upset and find a solution before a really big argument begins.

Sometimes kids think that it's the adults who ask to have the meetings, but I invite you to ask for a gathering too.

When my son was five, he really wanted to play a video game that some of his friends were playing. He had been frustrated that week about his dad and I not letting him play. Instead of arguing with us about it, though, he asked to have a mini gathering.

After we put his sister to sleep, we stayed up a little longer with him, and he told us all the reasons why he wanted to play the video game. We explained to him that in our home, we didn't let kids play video games at five. But we also told him that we would think about it for when he was older, and we were so proud of him for asking us to sit down and talk about something he felt was important. Now he is nine and does play some video games!

You can also talk to your grown-ups when *you* feel angry. They are learning tools in this book just like you are, and making time to check in as a family can save you from a lot of silly arguments.

# TOOL #4: WRITE OR DRAW IT OUT

Sometimes you just need a break, right? And sometimes we adults forget that you kids need a minute to relax.

Grab a pencil, pen, or some crayons, and use the space below to write about how you are feeling, draw a picture, or both.

This is your space to be creative!

If your grown-up has just asked you to do something (like clean up your room), see if you can find a solution. Maybe you can clean up half of your room, take a writing/drawing break for five minutes, and then finish cleaning after you are done.

Because this chapter is all about having fewer arguments in your home, this tool is here to help you when you need to get big feelings out so that you can come back to finding solutions with your grown-ups and listening to what needs to happen next.

# TOOL #5: OFFER OR ASK FOR A HUG

One of the best ways to stop an argument is to offer a hug or ask for one. Sometimes we feel so mad that it can be hard to give or get a hug. Sometimes we feel bossed around and we don't like being told what to do.

I remember feeling that way a lot as a kid, and I still feel that way sometimes as a grown-up.

When my kids are getting upset, I try to always ask them if they want a hug. It makes the whole mood of our house change almost instantly. But the cool thing is, now my kids also ask me if I want a hug when I am getting upset.

Don't forget: we are never too old for hugs!

In the next chapter, we are going to learn tools for when we fight with a sibling. And, if you don't have a sibling, still read the chapter because you can use the same tools with your friends!

With love,

Laura

# CHAPTER 3

# THE GOLDEN CHILD

Some days, parenting feels like getting pounded by wave after wave right at the shore of your favorite tropical beach; you know if you could just get out of the water, there would be warm sand and blissful sunshine ready to fill your day with happiness.

In many of those parenting moments when you feel the heaviness of the waves, you do eventually escape and get safely back to shore (yay!). You reconnect with your child, and you are back in the joy of parenting.

But if you have more than one child, you often discover within minutes of reaching shore that a brewing tropical storm is dumping down on you, your beach bag, and your sun hat (sigh!).

This is what sibling fighting feels like. First you work so very hard to help each of your children with their own needs and then, right when you hit a sweet spot, your kids start fighting and all you want to do is yell, cry, or escape.

Siblings need tools to diffuse their rivalries, change their behavior, and more effectively problem-solve so that they can enjoy smoother terrain along their journey.

By far my greatest parenting challenge has been sibling rivalry. This is not because my children fight constantly or are particularly harsh with each other. It is because I grew up as an only child, so the world of sibling rivalry was very new to me. (And if you have an only child, don't skip this chapter, because these tools will help with peer-to-peer arguments as well.)

In my childhood, my interactions with kids were from my peer group. And, for the most part, we all got along quite well (or at least didn't fight as much as siblings do). So, sibling bickering, hitting, and overall frustrations were something I was unaccustomed to.

My husband, on the other hand, is one of four boys. I always appreciate his perspective when our children argue because he grew up in a home where sibling discourse was normalized.

Because I didn't have direct sibling experience growing up, I had a big learning curve when my kids got old enough to argue. What that looked like for me was reading many parenting books on the subject, talking to professionals in the field, looking for the research that was most effective, and trying out various tools with my own two children when they fought.

I have noticed that over time, my children have fought less. I have also noticed what a strong bond they have now at seven and nine. I take this as a personal testament to the tools I have learned over the years about navigating this difficult aspect of parenting and the work we have done on sibling kindness in our home.

Sibling rivalry is normal. All siblings will fight, but for their long-term relationship, what's most important is for their connection and good times to outweigh the bad moments.

We can help create a home that better nurtures our children's relationship so that they have stronger bonds in both the short-term and long-term.

So, let's work together to crawl out of the pounding waves and onto the peaceful beach, where an umbrella is waiting to protect you from any potential rain.

# TOOL #1: FAIR TREATMENT

**Fair (adjective):** *Being free of bias or injustice.*[8]

I was sitting at the kitchen table drawing with my two children when I glanced over at the picture my oldest had just finished. He has always been a talented artist and will spend hours practicing his drawing skills.

Admiring his work, I turned to him. "Oliver, I love the way that you drew that picture!" I said with great joy and zest.

My daughter looked up at me with big eyes and said, "So you like Oliver more?"

"Of course not," I said, taken aback. "I love you both the same."

My daughter sulked. I could tell she wasn't fully convinced.

In my many moments of pondering parenting, I have wondered about how praising one child can make the other feel unloved. How one child is treated as the "golden child," while the other one is seen as less than (or, even if that is not the true feelings of the adult, the child still believes it is so).

It is not always easy to treat children fairly, and the very idea can be confusing. Does fair treatment mean that you cannot comment on one of your children doing well? If your oldest child needs new shoes, must you buy all your children new shoes even if the younger ones don't need them?

Below I share some tools for how you can best navigate treating siblings fairly.

## NAVIGATING FAIR TREATMENT

When we examine the tool of fair treatment in our home, we are really looking to fulfill two main components:

**1.** We treat our children fairly with the love, time, attention, and praise we give them.

**2.** When our children do fight, we speak to all of them in a fair way, without taking sides or making quick assumptions of who is to blame.

Let's first look at component number one: we treat our children fairly with the love, time, attention, and praise we give them.

To be clear, this tool does not pertain to things that one child may need. For example, when it comes to clothes, if one of my children needs new shoes and the other one doesn't yet, I will not necessarily buy shoes for the one who does not need them.

I think it is healthy for children to not always get something just because a sibling needs something (this can be a good learning opportunity to talk about needs vs. wants, where money comes from in your family, and your values around how it is spent).

Similarly, if one of my children does well at something, I will share enthusiasm for their accomplishment openly (if appropriate) or privately. If I do share that praise openly in front of my other child, I am mindful of my other child's feelings. In the earlier example of my son's picture, I learned that my daughter is at an age where this kind of praise toward her brother brings up worries of my love for her. That was good feedback to get because it is something we actively work on (more on that in Chapter 7).

As my daughter is working on the skill of not comparing other's accomplishments to her own sense of worthiness, I may choose to take my son aside and look through his sketchbook when it is just the two of us. I will go through each picture with him and share my compliments with him openly.

In *Siblings Without Rivalry*, Adele Faber supports this point by writing, "Children often experience praise of a brother or sister as a put-down of themselves. They automatically translate, 'Your brother is so considerate' into 'Mom thinks I'm not.' It's a good idea to save our enthusiastic comments for the ear of the deserving child."

So, when we are examining fair treatment in terms of love, time, attention, and praise, the main goals are that you. . .

» Be mindful of showing love to each one of your children daily.

» Set up special times to connect and play with each one of your children that are fair in the amount of time and attention you give each of them.

» Be thoughtful of how your attention toward one child affects the other.

» Try to have a balanced approach.

» Look for ways to praise all your children (if one child is more difficult to find things to be praised about, you especially try to catch their good moments).

In the space below, please take a moment to respond to the following questions:

*Think of a time in your life when you felt like a sibling or friend was given more time and attention from someone you cared about. How did that make you feel?*

_____

_____

_____

*Think of a time when you may have treated one of your children like the "golden child" while punishing or blaming the other child. What do you think both children felt like in that moment? How did you feel after?*

_____

_____

_____

*Do you tend to show favoritism toward one of your children? If so, what actions can you take to strengthen your connection to your other child/children?*

_____

_____

_____

*Make a list of ten things that you find uniquely special about each of your children. If you want, share each list with your children.*

_____

_____

_____

*Upon your reflection, do you have a key takeaway? If so, write it below.*

_____

_____

_____

Now, let's examine the second component of this tool: when our children do fight, we speak to all of them fairly without taking sides or making quick assumptions of who is to blame.

Here is another quote by Adele Faber in *Siblings Without Rivalry*:

> "Imagine," I thought, "a world in which brothers and sisters grow up in homes where hurting isn't allowed; where children are taught to express their anger at each other sanely and safely; where each child is valued as an individual, not in relation to the others; where cooperation, rather than competition, is the norm; where no one is trapped in a role; where children have daily experience and guidance in resolving their differences."

I love this quote for many reasons. For this tool, it reminds us of the importance of giving fair treatment to our children when they fight rather than creating a cycle of blame toward one child. When we do this, we may nurture the sibling relationship and create a home environment that feels safe for all.

Now, let's look at two typical scenarios of sibling fighting.

## SCENARIO #1

You are downstairs cooking dinner when you are suddenly interrupted by the sound of crying, screaming, and stomping.

Frustrated that your children are fighting again, you take a moment to sit down at the kitchen table. You inhale for a count of 1, 2, 3, placing your hand on your belly or heart. Then, you exhale for a count of 1, 2, 3.

Again, you inhale for a count of 1, 2, 3.

Exhale for a count of 1, 2, 3.

On your way up the stairs, you gently remind yourself that this is an opportunity to help your children learn problem-solving tools.

When you walk into the room, you discover your younger daughter crying because her older sister took her favorite stuffed animal and pushed her when she asked for it back.

Calmly, you call a mini family gathering and ask both your children to sit on the ground.

After giving each child a hug, you say that you would like to hear what happened from both of them individually.

After listening to each side of the story, you ask them how they think they can solve this problem.

In the end, they decide to trade stuffed animals until dinner and then trade back before bedtime.

You applaud them for finding the solution and then circle back about the pushing. You talk to your older daughter about other tools she can use when she gets upset (hurting hands are never allowed).

If this has been an ongoing problem with pushing, you may consider a logical/natural consequence—perhaps writing a note apologizing to her little sister or asking her to play downstairs where you can keep a more watchful eye.

After talking with both children, you go back to cooking dinner.

## SCENARIO #2

You are downstairs cooking dinner when you are suddenly interrupted by the sound of crying, screaming, and stomping.

Immediately frustrated that your children are fighting, you walk upstairs to discover your younger daughter crying because her older sister took her favorite stuffed animal and pushed her when she asked for it back.

You grab the stuffed animal out of your older daughter's hands, give it to her crying sister, and tell them that if they fight one more time, there will be no dessert after dinner.

As you turn to leave the room, you look your older daughter in the eye and tell her, "I expect you to do better. You are the older sister."

With that, you march back downstairs to finish making dinner.

Now answer the following questions about the two scenarios.

*How did you feel as the adult reading the first scenario?*

_____

_____

*How do you think each child may have felt?*

_____

_____

*How did you feel as the adult reading the second scenario?*

_____

_____

*How do you think each child may have felt?*

_____

_____

When we look at our interactions through the lens of our children, it is easier to see why it is so important to take blame out of the equation and instead help our children work together to find a solution.

Treating children fairly will not only help in the moment of discord but also teach them how to navigate peer-to-peer frustrations and help them develop a deeper long-term bond with each other and friends.

# TOOL #2: BE PRESENT

As a parent of two, I have gone back and forth on how much I want to interfere when there is an argument and how much I should let my two children try to work it out themselves.

Of course, if there is any indication that a child may get hurt in an argument, it is extremely important to intervene right away.

As both your and your children's toolboxes continue to grow, it is nice to give children the space to practice their problem-solving and emotional regulation skills with each other.

I have found that there is a lot of power in helping to de-escalate an argument by simply being present.

Sometimes that looks like the above Scenario #1, where you step into the space, call a mini family gathering, and help your children work through their problem.

Being present can also look like you simply observing the argument from the doorway or sitting quietly on the floor. As your children become aware of your presence, it can become a cue for them to stop arguing and start using their tools.

You will gauge what being present looks like by the tone of the argument and how upset each child is.

However you show up, remember that your calming presence will set the tone within your home.

# TOOL #3: SPECIAL ONE-ON-ONE TIME

In the hustle of today's world, the reality is that we parents can always be working, socializing, and zoning out on our devices.

In a study published in *Pediatric Research*, assistant professor in human development and family science at Illinois State University Brandon McDaniel observed that the more parents were distracted by tech, the more kids acted out. But it didn't stop there; it became a cycle. As kids acted out, parents became stressed, and when parents were stressed, they turned to technology, which, of course, only led to more acting out.[9]

Our children suffer in cycles (more to come on this topic in Chapter 5) and, when it comes to sibling rivalry, having distracted parents can leave them feeling angry, diminished, and frustrated with their parents and siblings.

Then, when you add on siblings fighting with each other and parents taking sides or taking on the arguments themselves, this leads to tension within the home.

In an effort to minimize the hurt feelings that your children may very well be experiencing, I suggest having special one-on-one time each day with each child. I still suggest this even if you are a device-free home because it strengthens your bond, boosts happy hormones in everyone's brain, and contributes to a happy home!

Now, before you jump into fear that you don't possibly have enough time to have special one-on-one time, let me reassure you that this time doesn't have to be long.

You don't need to devote hours every day to playing with each of your children. You do, however, need to set aside at least ten minutes with no devices and be present to play, draw, talk, or listen.

In the kid's section, I am going to suggest that your children also carve out special one-on-one time to spend together each day. For this tool though, I am suggesting that *you* offer this time separately to each child.

As the classic saying goes, "the days are long, but the years are short."

I always have to remind myself that these years of raising my children are precious and connecting in a joyful way with each of my children every day is a gift!

After you have tried this for a while, take note if sibling rivalry seems to be reduced in your home. It is my theory that the more siblings feel secure in their attachment to you as the parent/caregiver, the less angry they get with each other.

# TOOL #4: PLAY TOGETHER AS A FAMILY

As mentioned, it's normal for children to fight, but the best predictor of a good relationship as adults is having more good memories together than bad.

This last tool will help you set the stage for your children to have more positive interactions and create happy childhood memories.

Here is a list of some of our favorite ways to play together as a family. Additionally, I am including a bonus tip on family camping (which is our most favorite way to spend larger chunks of family time together).

## FIVE FUN WAYS TO PLAY AS A FAMILY

**1.** Make cookies and build a fort in the living room to eat them in.

**2.** Play board games that are age appropriate (I also bring cards in my purse so we can always play a round of go fish or gin rummy).

**3.** Let your children make up an imaginary game and tell you what character they want you to be.

**4.** Build with Lego or blocks, or make something new out of cardboard boxes.

**5.** Get out the arts and crafts supplies and create together.

## BONUS: FAMILY CAMPING!

Truth time: I am an avid camping enthusiast, and I believe it has been one of the healthiest rituals our family has created.

When our children turned two and four, my husband and I decided it was time to start camping. We had always dreamed of buying a trailer that could hook up to our car, so we purchased our first 16-foot trailer, squeezed our daughter's pack-n-play into the narrow walkway, and fumbled as we learned how to navigate the trailer on our first adventure.

To say the least, we were rusty. . .but since that first camping trip, we have made an effort to camp once a month, and most months we make it out for at least one or two nights.

Over the past five years, we have learned a lot about camping with kids. Today, I am sharing some of my favorite camping tips in the hope they will inspire you to get out in nature and explore.

If you aren't ready for a full weekend camping trip, don't despair. You can start by pitching a tent in the backyard of your own home or a friend's house.

## Five Tips for a Calmer Camping Trip

**1.** Plan meals ahead: Meals are always the most stressful part of camping for me. I want to make sure that I bring enough food, but I don't want to pack the whole kitchen sink. In the past year, I have started meal planning before our camping trips, and it has been a lifesaver.

My tip for meal planning is to find a few ingredients that will work for multiple meals. For example, carrots will go in my tin foil dinner packets (carrots, potatoes, and ground beef), they will be part of our big salad lunch (lettuce with lots of veggies, seeds, and garbanzo beans), and they will also work sliced with dressing for the second dinner of the trip (usually hotdogs or tofu pups). The lettuce that I bring for the salad will go in sandwiches on the third day of our trip and the leftover seeds will go into a trail mix for snacks. Having an overview of your daily menu will save you a lot of time and energy once you arrive on your trip.

**2.** Bring layers and an extra trash bag for dirty clothes: Camping with kids means dirty clothes, and often, warm days turn quickly into cold nights (especially in California, where we lived until 2021 and did a lot of our camping). Be prepared with layers so that your children can keep playing while you are cooking dinner over the fire. Reuse clothes for as long as possible but have an extra-large trash bag nearby so that clothes can easily be saved for the washing machine when you return home. And always be safe and check clothes and kids for ticks and bugs before bed.

**3.** Have a special camping toy bag: We have a bag of toys that lives with our camping gear. We never bring the toys into our house so that they stay novel for our trips. They include outdoor toys like binoculars, a bug-catching kit, buckets, and a pretend camping stove. We also have a few books for reading at bedtime and stuffed animals for snuggling with.

This is also a great place to put any extra gifted toys you might not want in your own home: kinetic sand, play dough, and silly putty are a few that live in our camping toy bag!

**4.** Tent camping 101: If you are camping in a tent, bring a comfortable mattress and extra layers to put on top of your sleeping bag. Remember that temperatures drop at night, so be prepared for chilly nights. Also, keep a flashlight on hand with a pair of flip flops next to the tent door for middle-of-the-night bathroom trips.

**5.** Have fun: Dig in the dirt, search for bugs, and don't be afraid to let your kids stay up a little later than normal. I grew up camping with my mom! We traveled all over California, exploring natural hot springs, hiking through meadows of butterflies, seeing bears crossing through our campsites, and making new friends everywhere we went. Some of my favorite childhood memories are our camping trips together.

Camping is a time to let loose and not worry about dirty hands or staying up late for extra stories. Every camping trip we take is a time for our family to bond, and we cherish letting the kids be a little wilder on these trips than we normally are at home.

Embrace and tap into *your* wild side! You are making memories with your family that will last a lifetime.

## Laura's Favorite Camping Meals for a Three-Day Camping Trip

- ❏ Hot dogs or tofu pups
- ❏ Steak, chicken, or plant-based meat
- ❏ Ground beef or plant-based meat
- ❏ Eggs
- ❏ Cheese
- ❏ Red peppers
- ❏ Zucchini
- ❏ Onions
- ❏ Yellow squash
- ❏ Carrots
- ❏ Red potatoes
- ❏ Bread
- ❏ Oatmeal
- ❏ Extra snacks and bottled water
- ❏ BBQ sauce and/or ketchup
- ❏ Hummus
- ❏ Aluminum foil

*Read the directions below to see how many of the ingredients go into several meals. You can plan quantities according to how many people are camping with you.

### THREE-DAY CAMPING TRIP MENU

|  | Breakfast | Lunch | Dinner |
|---|---|---|---|
| Day 1 | N/A | N/A | Tofu pups or hot dogs roasted over the fire. Pair this with sliced red peppers and zucchini that you can also roast over the fire. |
| Day 2 | Scrambled eggs with veggies and cheese. Veggies can be zucchini, red peppers, onions, and yellow squash. | Sandwiches with sliced carrots and hummus. | Tinfoil packets with sliced red potatoes, carrots, red pepper, and ground beef or plant-based meat. Place the ingredients inside tinfoil packets and cook them over fire. I like to serve these packets with BBQ sauce or ketchup. |
| Day 3 | Oatmeal. | Sandwiches again. | (Optional for if you stay later) Tinfoil fajita packets with sliced red pepper, zucchini, onions, and steak, chicken, or plant-based meat. Create packets just like you did on Day 2, and cook them over the fire. |

# FOR YOUR KIDS

For kids, having a sibling can sometimes feel like a competition. Someone is the "golden child," and someone is the "trouble child." Sibling A is neat and organized; sibling B is messy and chaotic. Sibling A is well-behaved. Sibling B doesn't share.

For children, we can help them understand that each sibling is allowed to be different, that fighting is normal, that solving conflict is part of being human, and that they are all equally loved and valued.

With the unique and useful tools in this chapter, children will learn to problem-solve on their own and work through their rivalries to foster closer connection and a deeper relationship.

The remaining part of this chapter can now be read aloud to your child.

**Dear Friends,**

How are you doing with your problem-solving toolbox so far? Have you liked any of the tools you have been learning? In the box below, I invite you to draw a picture of a time you used one of your tools from Chapter 1 or Chapter 2. If you don't remember the tools you are learning, ask your grown-up to go back and share a few with you now.

In this chapter, I'm going to share some tools that will help you when you are arguing with a sibling or friend.

If you have a sibling, you know how easily a fight can start between you. That is very normal between siblings.

You also know how fun it can be to play with your sibling when you are getting along and how you can have the best time making up games, telling jokes, or playing outside in the backyard.

I want to help you have more fun and argue less. You can do that using the tools you have already learned and adding a few more.

# TOOL #1: PLAN PLAYTIME

When my kids were younger, it seemed like they never wanted to play together at the same time. My daughter would want to play Legos, but her brother would want to rest in his room. Then my son would be ready to play, only to discover that my daughter was engaged in an art project alone.

They would feel frustrated that the times that they wanted to play weren't the same for both of them.

That is when we discovered that planning a time to play was just the tool they needed at home!

Just like you plan a playdate with a friend on the weekend or ask to find a time to hang at the park with a kid from class after school, planning playtime with your sibling can really help create time together that is special and fun.

If you need to, ask your grown-up to help you figure out a time each day that you and your sibling are free from after-school activities and can have some special playtime together. In our house, ten to twenty minutes before bed is always a really nice time for our kiddos to play.

Of course, this doesn't have to be the only time you get to play with your sibling. You can play as often as you want (that is the fun of having a sibling!), but knowing you will have uninterrupted playtime each day can help strengthen the special connection you have.

# TOOL #2: CREATE A PROJECT TOGETHER

Having a project that you and your sibling are doing together can give you something to look forward to and focus on.

It is easier to slip into arguments about what activity each person wants to play or who is going to be what character in the imaginary game that you both just made up. Although those are great ways to play and I invite you to play that way often, I also would love to suggest that you find a project you and your sibling can do for several days or weeks. If you don't have a sibling, this can also be a nice activity to do with a neighborhood friend or your grown-up.

Would you like to build a fort out of cardboard boxes?

Would you like to create a book that you can publish at the local copy shop?

Would you like to make bracelets with beads to sell at a lemonade stand?

Or what about turning old office supplies into a fun workstation?

There are endless possibilities of projects you can create with your sibling(s)!

A craft that my two children enjoy doing together is making soy wax candles. Their dad and I help them with parts of it because wax is very hot, but they mix, scoop, pour, and design the candles mostly on their own! They even sell the candles and give part of what they earn to help animals and people in need.

Why don't you use the space below to make a list or draw a picture of some of the projects you would like to do? Then, you can compare ideas with your sibling or friend and find something you both think would be fun. Maybe you could even work on your project during your planned playtime.

# TOOL #3: KINDNESS BOX

In Tool #4 (which is coming up next!), you will find a list of some of my favorite picture books to help grow kindness and make good choices with your siblings and peers.

One of the books on the list is called *Have You Filled a Bucket Today?* by Carol McCloud.

The book is about how everyone has an invisible bucket that they carry around. When you are kind to someone, you are being a bucket filler, which makes the other person feel happy and you feel happy too.

When you are hurtful toward someone, you take away from their bucket, and that takes away from your bucket too.

When you practice kindness in your family, it fills your family's bucket and your own.

One way to practice kindness is to give appreciation to the people that you love.

Appreciation is telling someone something you like about them or giving thanks for something that they did.

For this tool, you can make a kindness box for each one of your siblings (you can also make one for your grown-ups if you want).

An old shoe box is great for making a kindness box. You can decorate the sides with stickers and glitter glue. Then, you can ask a grown-up to cut a slit along the top of the box.

After dinner each night, have each person write a note of appreciation and put it in the box. At the end of the week, open the boxes and read all the notes of appreciation you have for each other aloud.

The more we focus on the things we love about our siblings, the easier it will be to get along and play well together! Plus, it feels so good to hear what people appreciate about you and to share what you love about them.

# TOOL #4: FIVE AWESOME PICTURE BOOKS

Here are five of my favorite picture books that will support you with the tools you are learning and give you some extra ideas too!

**1.** *Have You Filled a Bucket Today?* by Carol McCloud

**2.** *Carmela Full of Wishes* by Matt de la Peña

**3.** *What Does It Mean to Be Kind?* by Rana DiOrio

**4.** *Be Kind* by Pat Zietlow Miller

**5.** *What Should Danny Do?* by Ganit Levy and Adir Levy

Look for these books at your local library or bookstore, or see if you may have a copy in your classroom that you can borrow!

You now have four powerful tools to help you nurture your sibling bond and, like I said, you can use these same tools with a friend if you are an only child.

Keep up the good work. I will share more fun activities with you in the next chapter!

With love,

Laura

# CHAPTER 4

# WORRY IS NOT YOUR FRIEND

I had just been invited to take newborn baby pictures with my son. I was teaching first grade at the time, and one of the moms in the class offered to photograph us.

I was so excited to go to the photo shoot, which we planned to model after the famous photos of Anne Geddes (you know, the sleepy baby photos where each baby looks like they are sleeping in a flower, snuggled up in a watering bucket, or snoozing like a teddy bear).

Arriving at the studio, I was nervous because my son was one of those babies who didn't seem to sleep as much as all the other babies I knew. In fact, on many of my wakeful nights with him, I would rock him in my arms wondering who in the world coined the term "sleeping like a baby." Obviously, not a parent who had a child like mine!

I knew that getting those adorable pictures would require my son to sleep. During the shoot, it quickly became apparent that no naps were going to happen.

I was embarrassed that the Anne Geddes picture plans weren't panning out. Then, to boot, the photographer mom let me borrow one of her dresses for the shoot, which my son *urinated* on!

I left the studio feeling self-conscious (which I now understand is a very normal feeling for first-time mothers) and wondering if this mom was upset about her dress.

Time passed, and I didn't hear anything about the pictures. My mind started to fill with worry. Was she upset with me? Was she disappointed that we couldn't do the shoot like she wanted? Did I need to call her and check? Should I offer to dry-clean her dress? Would she tell the other moms in the class that I couldn't get my child to nap?

My worries weren't rational, and although part of me knew that, I couldn't drop the obsession. And it really felt just like that: an *obsession*.

I wasn't a stranger to worry, per se, but ever since I had become a mother, I was aware that fear was starting to navigate my decisions rather than coming along for the ride. And, in my heart, I knew that I couldn't let my fears start to take over like that.

Elizabeth Gilbert said it perfectly in *Big Magic: Creative Living beyond Fear*:

"It seems to me that the less I fight my fear, the less it fights back. If I can relax, fear relaxes too."

Gilbert was right. Fear is really just False Evidence Appearing Real. I was mistaking *fear* for *fact*. I had to incorporate better strategies (and fast).

For the photography snafu, everything turned out fine between me and the photographer mom, and my fear was simply that—*fear*.

The mom had been on vacation for a weekend and then had a family emergency that came up. She wasn't upset about the photo shoot (in fact, the pictures turned out terrific), and her dress was easily washed.

I was relieved that there had been a good outcome, but I was keenly aware of the larger issue at hand and began to do some deeper work. My worry was taking away my serenity, and I needed strategies and tools to decrease the fear that was trying to dominate my mind.

Attending a lecture at a Zen Center in Northern California, I learned that most people have fifty thousand to sixty thousand thoughts per day. Since then, I have read articles that estimate that number to be higher and other articles that say we have around six thousand thoughts per day.[10] If we are conservative in our estimate for the number of thoughts we have per day and keep it at six thousand, that is still a lot of thoughts! Many of these thoughts are repetitive in nature, focused on past mistakes and rooted in future worry. If that weren't enough, parents have the extra stress of worrying about their children's physical and mental well-being.

And now, since 2019 and counting, we have all experienced a global pandemic, which has brought worry to a whole new level.

Of course, some worry is normal, but as parents we often experience phases of worry that will keep us up at night, distract us from being present with our children, and keep our minds racing.

Worry doesn't have to be the captain of the ship anymore; yes, it is part of our experience, but it shouldn't take over. We deserve to be equipped with the many tools we didn't learn as children, and we can begin to teach our children now.

Below I offer five powerful tools that have helped me tame worries. I know they can help you too. It is important to reduce our worrying (and ultimately our stress) because when our minds are lost in worries, we are more short-tempered and reactive with our children. When we learn to quiet that part of the brain, we find that our reactivity will decrease as well.

# TOOL #1: DOT ACTIVITY

After coming to terms with my worry and realizing I needed to take some action around it, I signed up for a one-day meditation retreat at the local Zen center and brought my good friend along.

At the retreat, the meditation teacher told each of us to take a piece of paper and a pencil. He set a timer for two minutes. Each time we had a thought, we should make a dot on our paper.

I will now invite you to take out a piece of paper and a pencil, find a quiet space to sit, and set a timer for two minutes.

Every time you have a thought, make a dot on your paper (note: thinking about *not* having a thought counts as a thought!).

After the timer is done, look at your paper. Are you surprised to see how many thoughts you could think in two minutes? I was surprised the first time I did this exercise!

The human mind is busy, and we see that when we do this dot activity. In fact, I love doing this activity because it reminds me of the true nature of the mind: busy, worried, and untamed at times.

When I give myself space from my thoughts and observe them like the dots on the paper, I am less affected by what each worry is saying to me.

This tool helps to detach from the fret of the mind.

# TOOL #2: WRITE IT OUT AND RIP IT UP

Sometimes worry just needs to be heard. Try as you might to push it away or ignore it, the worries just want to be acknowledged.

During these overwhelming moments, it can be helpful to talk to a friend, therapist, or spiritual teacher.

Other times though, simply letting every single thought pour out of you and onto a piece of paper can be just what you need to move through the fear.

For this tool, take out a piece of paper (or two or three) and free the worries onto the page. Write until you can't write anymore. Let every fear you have been carrying around run wild along the pages. And, if you feel like crying or yelling while you write, please go right ahead!

After you have written it all down, release it. Give yourself permission to let go of the fears and start ripping up the paper you just wrote on.

With each rip, lovingly detach from your fear. Know that the fear may not disappear completely, but you have now given yourself more space to let good thoughts and feelings come in.

After you are done with this tool, I invite you to sit for a few minutes with your hand on your heart. Be proud of yourself for practicing this work and kind to yourself for carrying the burden of your worries.

# TOOL #3: GET TO THE ROOT

This is another writing exercise for you to do when worry comes to visit. To apply it, write down your main worry, then get to the root of the worry by asking, "If that is true, then what does that mean?"

A friend taught me this tool over a decade ago, and it has served me well for all these years.

I like to think of worry as the same little creature that always shows up with a different disguise. Worrying is tricky like that because it seems that your worries are new each time, so you take them very seriously. The truth, though, is that most fears tend to lead back to the same root worry.

Let me give you an example.

Imagine there is a new group of moms at your child's school, and they have just started to organize morning hikes.

Two of your other mom friends have been invited on the hikes, but you haven't heard anything.

You are worried that these other moms must not like you and that is why you haven't been invited. Furthermore, you are also now concerned that if you are not included on these hikes, your child will not be invited to as many playdates or weekend birthday parties.

Using the Get to the Root tool, you decide to write down your main worry:

Fear of not being invited on morning hikes.

Now, you can ask yourself this question: "If that is true, then what does that mean?"

You write: If I am not being invited on morning hikes, then that would mean that the other moms don't like me.

Again, ask yourself this question: "If that is true, then what does that mean?"

You write: If the other moms don't like me, then my son won't be invited on playdates, and he will feel left out just like I do.

Again, ask yourself this question: "If that is true, then what does that mean?"

You write: If my son isn't invited on playdates, then our family won't be happy. We will be excluded from the community.

Again, ask yourself this question: "If that is true, then what does that mean?"

You write: If we are excluded from the community, then I will be alone, and I hate being alone. I will be excluded just like I often felt excluded as a kid.

Again, ask yourself this question: "If that is true, then what does that mean?"

You write: If I am excluded, then it means that there is something wrong with me. I am unlovable.

Now, my friend, you have reached the root of the fear: the fear of being unlovable (aka low self-worth).

Let's look at another example of this same fear wearing a different disguise.

Imagine that you and your child get in a fight, and your child tells you that they hate you.

That night, when you are going to bed, you can't help but feel crushed by the anger and harsh words of your kid.

Using the Get to the Root tool, you decide to write down your main worry: my child will continue to talk meanly and doesn't appreciate me.

Now, you can ask yourself this question: "If that is true, then what does that mean?"

You write: If my child talks meanly to me, he will talk meanly to others. If he doesn't appreciate me, then he will continue to be mean to me and we will have an awful relationship.

Again, ask yourself this question: "If that is true, then what does that mean?"

You write: If we have an awful relationship, he will reject me. If he is mean to others, he will be rejected by them.

Again, ask yourself this question: "If that is true, then what does that mean?"

You write: If my child is rejected and rejecting, then I am not raising my child right. There is something that I am doing wrong as a parent.

Again, ask yourself this question: "If that is true, then what does that mean?"

You write: If I am doing something wrong as a parent, then that means that I am bad at my most important job.

Again, ask yourself this question: "If that is true, then what does that mean?"

You write: If I am bad at my most important job, then that means I am basically failing. It means that I am a bad mom. It means that I am not *good*.

And there you have the same root issue of feeling unlovable (aka having low self-worth).

Of course, your root worries may be different from these two examples. The important takeaway in this tool is to identify the underpinning worries that take hold and create narratives that are untrue.

Once we start to see a common theme among our worries, we can start to dive into tools that support overcoming those deeper fears (more on this in later).

# TOOL #4: POSITIVE AFFIRMATIONS

Positive affirmations are positive statements that can be used to challenge negative thoughts or beliefs.

Examples of positive affirmations are:

» I am brave.

» I am loving toward myself and others.

» I am grateful to be a parent.

» I am worthy.

» I love myself.

Positive affirmations have become increasingly popular in recent years. Some people swear by them, and others think they are beyond cheesy.

Personally, I wasn't fully convinced that positive affirmations would combat my worry until I started researching the science behind them and devoting a daily practice to saying positive affirmations aloud or in my head each day.

Over time, I have seen the power that positive affirmations have to combat negative thoughts.

## FIVE IMPORTANT POINTS ABOUT POSITIVE AFFIRMATIONS

**1.** Affirmations are statements that we repeat to ourselves out loud or in our thoughts. They are self-suggestions. Repeat an affirmation frequently enough and it becomes hardwired into your belief system and helps form your identity (who you believe you are).[11]

**2.** Science, yes. Magic, no. Positive affirmations require regular practice if you want to make lasting, long-term changes to the ways that you think and feel. The good news is that the practice and popularity of positive affirmations are based on widely accepted and well-established psychological theory.[12]

**3.** A study published in the journal *Social Cognitive and Affective Neuroscience* revealed what goes on in our brains when we practice affirmations regularly. The researchers used MRI to find that practicing self-affirmation activates the reward centers in the brain. Thus, practicing self-affirmation does help make you happy and positive.[13]

**4.** The wonder of affirmations is that they hijack these cognitive biases for your own benefit. They teach your brain a new way to think about the world. If you repeat phrases to convince your brain that you'll get the job or achieve that target healthy weight, then your brain starts to subconsciously search for signs that will make this true. When it does, the brain will then present the sign to the conscious mind. All of a sudden, you'll begin noticing "points and proofs" that'll help you to achieve your goals. The affirmations just need time to help your brain tune in to the good stuff.14

**5.** Positive self-talk is a research-backed method of scaling to the upper echelons of Maslow's hierarchy of needs: self-esteem and self-actualization. Social scientist Claude Steele was the first to propose the theory of self-affirmation, which states that if people can feel relatively positive about themselves in one arena, they can better tolerate a threat to their self-integrity in another. More recently, MRI evidence suggests neural pathways increase when people practice self-affirmation. This provides a neurological basis for the idea that affirmations can help us develop a more optimistic way of looking at ourselves that persists.[15]

I encourage you to write down ten possible positive affirmations in the space below. Use one or two of them each day or rotate between them each month as needed.

1. _____

2. _____

3. _____

4. _____

5. _____

6. _____

7. _____

8. _____

9. _____

10. _____

# TOOL #5: RELEASING FEARS: GUIDED MEDITATION

We will take a deeper dive into meditation later in the book, when I will share the research, science, and benefits of having a meditation practice. For now, though, I invite you to sit with me as I take you through a mini guided meditation to help release your worry.

**1.** Find a comfortable seated position or lie with your back on the ground.

**2.** If you are seated in a chair, I suggest planting your feet on the floor or sitting with your back straight and your legs crisscrossed.

**3.** Inhale through your nose for a count of three. If you would like, place a hand on your belly and feel it rise as the air moves into the space.

**4.** Slowly release the breath through your nose or mouth for a count of three.

**5.** Repeat this until your body starts to feel calmer and you notice your inhales and exhales are smoother.

**6.** Now, I want you to imagine that each worry you have is going inside of a cloud. Carefully place your first worry inside of the cloud and allow the wind to blow it away through the sky.

**7.** As you visualize your worry floating away, I invite you to place a hand on your heart.

What do you need to tell yourself as this worry leaves? Perhaps you need reassurance and support? Perhaps you need to tell yourself that you're proud of this important work that you are doing? Be compassionate and kind as you allow your worry to sail away.

If you have another worry, you can repeat the visualization with the same self-compassionate thoughts.

As you return now to your inhales and exhales, notice how your body feels. Is there anywhere in your body that feels lighter and less tense?

Pema Chödrön, the first American woman to become a fully ordained Buddhist nun in the Tibetan tradition, says, "You are the sky. Everything else—it's just the weather."

Throughout my day when I do this guided meditation, I take this quote with me to remind myself that I am simply observing the changing world around me (in meditation practice, we call this bringing equanimity[16] to what occurs throughout each day).

Repeat this practice for as long as you need to in order to sink deeper into the release of fear and the practice of self-compassion.

Worry can keep children from fully engaging in activities at school and at home. Worry deters them from trying new things: learning to swim, riding a bike, or having a sleepover at a friend's house—just to name a few. Worry can also lead our little ones to feel separate from their peers and embarrassed by the fears that they believe only they harbor inside.

When I taught elementary school, I worked with many children who were limited by their worries. I empowered them with the same tools I will share in this chapter (plus more that I have since learned).

Since my formal teaching days in school, I have worked with many parents, exploring their children's fears and finding practical solutions to help them navigate through them.

As you know from Chapter 1, when my daughter was five, we had an unknown mold problem in our home that greatly affected her immune system and caused extreme anxiety in her life. It was at that point that I brought all my tools for fearful thinking together and created a toolbox for her that was so big, her doctors gasped in amazement at her progress.

With the help of the tools I will share next and by clearing the mold out of her system, she went from a severely anxious five-year-old to an independent and high-functioning six-year-old.

This chapter is designed for the worrying child with stories about the brain, wonderful picture book suggestions, and important sensory skills to add to their growing toolbox.

The rest of the chapter will now be written for your child/children.

**BREAK FREE FROM REACTIVE PARENTING**

# FOR YOUR KIDS

**Dear Friends,**

When I was in fifth grade, my class went to Walker Creek for our long-awaited school sleepover. I had been looking forward to the overnight adventure for months and was so excited to bunk with my friends and be away from home for a night.

The day finally arrived, and I proudly loaded up my duffle bag and set off for nature walks, a class dance, and yummy meals to share with my friends.

I was assigned to a small cabin with four girls. There were two bunk beds in the room, and I quickly called "top bunk" and carried my stuff up the ladder.

Everything seemed to be going well until, all of a sudden, my worry set in. My eyes began to fill with tears. My vision became blurry. I could feel my hands getting hot and my heart beating a bit faster. I missed my mom, and I was worried that I would miss her for the whole night!

My friends asked me what was wrong, and being too embarrassed to tell them, I pretended I was upset about forgetting my hairbrush.

The truth is that in fifth grade, I had no tools to deal with my worry. What I know now is that my friends would have happily supported me if I had told them the truth. What I also know is that there are so many great tools to help with worry and lots of other kids experience worry just like I did.

I would like to add some tools to your toolbox for when your mind worries. It is normal to have fears (everyone does), but the cool thing that lots of people don't know about is that you can learn to make your fears quieter (and sometimes go away completely).

# TOOL #1: WHAT DO YOU SEE, HEAR, SMELL, AND FEEL?

When your thoughts get caught in a loop of fear, start to notice what you see, hear, smell, and feel around you.

For example:

> I see a tree. I see a house. I see a cat. I see a blue flower.
>
> I hear my voice talking. I hear a dog barking. I hear a car driving fast.
>
> I can feel the grass under my feet. I feel the way the oak leaf is rough on the edges. I feel the beat of my heart.
>
> I smell the blue flower. I smell the grass.
>
> Want to go smell the lemon in the kitchen?
>
> This becomes calming as you continue to notice and say what you see, hear, smell, and feel.

As you do this, you might even notice that your mind starts to unhook from the worry that was taking over (it is a pretty cool tool in that way!).

Even if it only stops the worry for a short amount of time, that is still *awesome*. Keep practicing! It is kind of like riding a bike—the more you practice, the easier it gets.

# TOOL #2: NAME THE WORRY

When my daughter was five, she started to get really nervous. Well, nervous is probably not the right word; she was scared about almost everything. She was scared to swim, scared to go to school, scared for me to leave her with anyone else.

To help her with her fear, I taught her about the brain, just like you and your grown-up have been learning about the brain in this book!

Let's do a quick reminder of the brain now, to make sure we use this tool the best we can.

# BRAIN FACTS

**1.** The lower area of the brain has this important part called the amygdala. The amygdala looks like this:

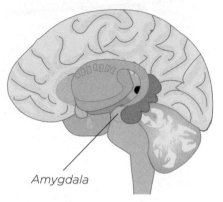

*Amygdala*

Human brain

This is the part of the brain that has a lot of important jobs, and one of them is knowing when to be in fear. It's good we have that amygdala because it can help keep us safe.

If you were being chased by a lion that escaped from the zoo, it would tell you to run away. Or, if a shark were swimming straight toward you, it would help you swim really, really, really fast.

But all silliness aside, we do need this part of the brain. The tricky thing is, sometimes the amygdala thinks we need to be worried about stuff that we don't actually have to be worried about (for example, my daughter being afraid to learn how to swim).

**2.** In the upper part of the brain, a lot of super-cool parts help us think about the choices we make, how other people feel, how we feel, and much more.

One of those amazing parts of the brain is called the prefrontal cortex. It looks like this:

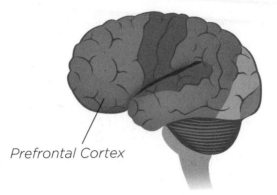

*Prefrontal Cortex*

Human brain

This part of the brain can help us make wise choices. It can help us remember that many of the things we think are really scary are actually fun and safe (again, like learning to swim).

So, in this tool, you can either make up a name for your amygdala and your prefrontal cortex or use the scientific names like we have been doing so far.

If you want to make up a name, I have a few suggestions.

| **Names for Your Amygdala** | **Names for Your Prefrontal Cortex** |
|:---:|:---:|
| Frank the Fearful | Wally the Wise |
| Francine the Fearful | Wendy the Wise |
| The Worried Mind | The Mindful Mind |
| The Fearful Mind | The Wise Mind |

No matter what you call these parts of your brain, the important part of the tool is telling a grown-up or yourself when you notice that the amygdala is being really loud.

When my daughter went through her fears, she would tell me that *Francine the Fearful* was really loud in her mind. To which I would ask, "What does your *Wise Mind* say?"

It was incredible how just labeling those parts of the mind would help her immediately calm down and get back to a place where she could see that her fear wasn't as scary as it was pretending to be.

I hope you will try this neat trick.

Also, if you want to read a good picture book that talks about the different parts of the brain and how they work, my kids and I love *The Animals in My Brain* by Sarah Joseph.

# TOOL #3: BIG BREATHS

We talk about the breath in many parts of this book because the breath is an amazing tool, and it is really easy to use.

The only frustrating thing about using the breath is these days, lots of adults have made the mistake of telling kids a lot to "take a deep breath and calm down!"

Even though grown-ups usually mean well when they say that, it can make kids feel like taking a deep breath is some sort of a punishment or one more thing that you have to do.

We don't want that!

Your breath is your power (just like it became Wolf's power in the story on page 32).

Scientists think the breath is so cool that they actually study it. What they have found is that taking just six deep breaths can majorly calm your body and mind down.

So let's make deep breathing fun; instead of being a "have to," it can be a "get to"!

## FIVE FUN WAYS TO USE YOUR BREATH

**1.** Place your hands over the sink and put a little bit of dish soap in them. Let them get sudsy with water and see if you can blow bubbles through your fingers.

**2.** Place a stuffed animal on your belly and watch it rise and fall with the inhale and exhale of your breath.

**3.** Make a cup of tea with lemon and honey. Softly blow the steam off the top to cool the tea down.

**4.** Ask a grown-up to put up ten fingers and pretend each finger is a birthday candle that you get to blow out. Then, switch, and have them blow your candles out.

**5.** If it is safe to do so, ask a grown-up if they can light a candle for you to blow out. Can they do this a few times? How does it feel to blow the flame out? What does the smoke look like? What does it smell like? Remember, this should only be done with an adult there to help you. It is never safe to be with fire alone.

# TOOL #4: PRACTICE AND THEN PRACTICE AGAIN

Worry is interesting because it wants to make you afraid so you never do or try the thing you are scared of.

Like we talked about earlier, sometimes this worry is really good. We don't ever want to put our hands on a hot stove because we would get burned. We never want to play with fire because we could get hurt or start a big fire. We never want to play with a knife because the sharp edge could stab us.

But, then, worry talks about other things in our minds that we don't actually need to be afraid of. Maybe it says it is too scary to spend the night at a friend's house. Worry might tell you to avoid doing the class play in front of an audience. It might say that going to a new school is too scary. Or, perhaps, just like my daughter experienced, the worry says not to practice swimming.

When these kinds of worries boss you around, they aren't really protecting you. And there is a really good way to move past those worries so you can try new things and have fun experiences. The tool is to practice what you fear (and then practice some more).

Let me give you an example from when I helped my daughter not only try swim lessons, but also learn to be one of the best seven-year-old swimmers I know (in fact, on our last camping trip to the Yuba River, someone gave her a reward because she dove to the bottom of the river and found their favorite sunglasses! She is a fish!).

My daughter was in swim class. All the other tots her age were dunking their heads in the water and splashing away. She refused.

The swim teacher finally came up to me one day and said that she didn't think my daughter would be able to stay in the swim class if she couldn't get over her fear of putting her head under the water.

I knew she needed to start practicing her way through this worry (and fast!).

The first step was to place a few of her favorite plastic dolls in the bathtub and put their heads under the water. We pretended the dolls were pretty scared too, at first, but over time, they warmed up to the water and started diving, twirling, and flipping under the water.

The next step was for my daughter to practice swim class in the bathtub. She put on her goggles, and I pretended to be her swim teacher. Slowly, she started to put her head under the water. Yahoo!

Well, all that practice made her really brave. She even started putting her head under water in our hot tub! See how her practicing her worry made her worry start to go away? Way cool, right?

Finally, she went to swim class, excited to show her teacher what she had learned. All the other parents who had been watching her for months at swim class cheered for my new little fish.

The next weekend, we went to a birthday party at a pool, and the kids thought my daughter was one of the best swimmers. They kept asking her how she got so good.

You know what she said?

*Practice!*

# TOOL #5: CHANGING THE MOVIE IN YOUR MIND

When I was little, we had these things called VCRs. They were electronic boxes that you could put a movie (which was an actual rectangular tape) in, and it would play on the TV. Maybe you have seen one?

Today, when my kids want to watch a movie, we usually use a DVD player, or we pick a movie from our Apple TV.

However you and your family watch movies these days, the point of this tool is to imagine that your worry is like a movie that is playing in your mind.

Sometimes, like I said before, we need that worry to keep us safe.

But when the worry is just causing trouble for us, we can imagine that we are taking the video out of the VCR player and putting in a new tape.

It can feel really good to know that you can change what you are paying attention to.

I did this the other day when I noticed I was worrying about getting all the laundry done in my house (sigh, I don't love doing laundry!).

I was worrying about when I would do my laundry. I was concerned about how long it would take. I worried I would be bored while I had to fold all the clothes.

Then, in the middle of the worry, I remembered that I didn't have to watch the Laundry Worry Movie! It isn't a good movie to watch.

Instead, I decided to put on a different mind movie. I picked a movie about gratitude that day. In that movie, I remembered that I was happy to have a family who helps me with the chores. I was lucky to have quiet time to myself at that moment. And I am always grateful to have this super-cool job where I get to connect with kids like you.

As my mind movie changed, so did the way I felt in my body. Instead of having an achy tummy and a tight jaw, I started to notice my body relax. My hands fell softly to my sides, and I took in a nice deep breath!

If you have fear, friends, I just want you to know that you are not alone. We all go through different times of worrying in our lives. When you find yourself in a place of worry, please keep coming back to these tools. You got this! And the worry will pass.

# CHAPTER 5

# WEAPONS OF MASS DISTRACTION

I had just finished reading to my daughter and putting her to bed. In the other room, I could hear my husband reading a chapter book to our son.

I walked into the living room and saw my phone and computer lying on the sofa. They were calling to me (like they so often do). They offered a chance to work on my book, to research parenting tools, or create more content to help support families. I *love* my work, and I look forward to every moment I get to sit down and dive deeper into it.

Technically speaking, I had already put one child to sleep. In our home, my husband and I alternate days reading to each kid and tucking them into bed. Because I'd put my daughter to sleep, I was "free" to sit and work.

And yet, my son was still awake. I debated my choices: Should I really not go in and say goodnight or give an extra snuggle just so I could be on my device?

I left my computer and phone sitting where they were and crept into my son's room. He immediately perked up and asked if I would cuddle in bed.

As we were lying there together, he put his head on my shoulder and told me how much he loves me and what a good mom he thinks that I am. Oh, those precious words! And to think, I could have missed all that.

Slowly, my son became sleepier and sleepier. I turned on my back and held his teddy bear in my arms. I was quiet as I stared up at the ceiling. Suddenly, noticing my stillness, my son rolled back over.

"Are you on your phone?" he asked. He peered at my hands, which were still holding his teddy bear. "Oh good," my son giggled. "I'm glad you aren't on your phone right now."

After a few more minutes of snuggling, he drifted to sleep. I wondered why he'd asked me that, but also knew that so often, I *am* on my phone when he's beside me.

Being on your phone is no longer an option; it's become an extended member of the family, another "entity" that our children have to compete with for our attention.

In this chapter we will learn tools for changing our relationship to our devices, for both ourselves and our children.

# TOOL #1: EXAMINING YOUR RELATIONSHIP WITH SCREENS

Over the years, we've heard so much in the media about children and screen time. This is a hugely important topic and one that we will definitely dive into in this chapter.

However, let's first examine our own relationships that we have to screens. Because let's face it—our phones are no longer a distraction; they're an addiction. This addiction to our devices keeps us from being truly present with our surroundings, our partners, our friends, our children and, ultimately, ourselves.

When devices take hold of our lives, our ability to self-regulate decreases (more on this shortly), and our reactivity to our children increases.

That is why it wouldn't be a proper reactive parenting book without addressing screen time. From the parents I see at school pick-up to the interviews I have done for *Good Day LA*, ABC News, *The Today Show*, and countless radio interviews, everyone seems to be asking the same questions: How much screen time is too much screen time for kids? What sort of screens are okay?

These are wonderful questions, but let's first begin by answering them for ourselves.

Take a moment to answer the questions below. Find a quiet space where you can really be honest with yourself as you reflect on each question.

**1.** *How often do you find yourself checking your phone each day? Take your best guess, or if you know how to look at your daily/ weekly screen time on your phone, see what it says and record the total time here.*

_____

**2.** *Do you find yourself checking your phone or being on a device when your child is trying to talk to you or get your attention?*

_____

**3.** *Do you check your phone first thing in the morning or right before bed?*

_____

**4.** *When you are overwhelmed with your family, do you notice you distract yourself with your phone?*

_____

**5.** *Has your child ever asked you to put your phone away?*

_____

**6.** *At night, after your kids go to bed, do you spend more time talking with another adult (such as your partner or a family member), or do you use that time to scroll through social media and/or turn on a movie/show?*

_____

**7.** *Do you ever leave your house without your phone with you?*

_____

**8.** *Are there times or spaces that you designate as phone-free? If yes, what are they? If no, would you want to have a phone-free zone? When, where, and for how long?*

_____

**9.** *True or False: You spend more time interacting with a device than with your child.*

_____

**10.** *Do you feel you have unhealthy habits around your devices? If yes, how would you like to change those habits?*

_____

**11.** *True or False: You often check your phone while on the toilet.*

_____

**12.** *Do you use devices as a way to dispel feelings of boredom?*

_____

**13.** *Do you use devices as a way to avoid feelings of sadness?*

_____

**14.** *On a scale of 1 to 10, how good do you feel after you scroll through social media? (1 being poor and 10 being really good)*

_____

**15.** *What benefits do your devices offer in your life? What are the consequences?*

_____

*After answering the questions above, write any key takeaways you have from this reflection. Would you like to set any new goals for yourself? Write your notes in the space provided below.*

_____

_____

_____

_____

_____

Admittedly, our devices have countless benefits in our lives—the ability to connect with friends and expand our social community, the option to work from home or anywhere in the world, access to important information communicated in a fast and efficient way, and the ability to learn more than we ever had access to before.

With that said, over the years, researchers have been studying and writing about the effects of devices on the parent-child relationship.

As parents become more engrossed, dependent, and engaged with their devices, it affects the time and energy they have to be present with their child.

My son asking me if I was on my phone as I snuggled him into bed was an important reflection for me personally to see how he must be perceiving my cell phone use. And, of course, it presented an opportunity to make changes within my own family system.

# TOOL #2: UNDERSTAND THE RESEARCH

I want to share with you how all of us can create healthier habits when it comes to screen time. But, first, let's examine what researchers are finding about the use of devices in the home.

» In October 2019, the New York Post reported on a study in which 2,000 parents of children 5 to 18 were polled about their use of devices with their children. The findings of the study showed that parents only spend 24 more minutes per day with their kids than their phones.[17] The study also revealed that children were asking parents to put their phones away, and 62 percent of participants shared that parents were spending too much time on their cell phone while with their kids.

» Another 2019 study reported in the *New York Times* said that "52 percent of parents said they spent too much time on mobile devices, nearly twice as many as in 2016."[18]

» In a 2016 study on how social media affects the parent-child relationship, California State University of San Bernardino reported, "Excessive use of social media has also shown to have effects on parenting; causing parental distraction, decreasing the level of everyday parental engagement, and making a child more likely to be at risk for injury."[19]

» A 2020 article by LifeWorks reported, "While parents are spending more time with their children than ever before, they aren't really present. They are glued to their phones, starving their children of the attention they need."[20]

» And a 2021 article in Verywell Family stated, "For every minute of time spent online, there is a cost: The negative impact of having less time for important things in your life such as sleep, leisure time, work, and family time."[21]

It is clear that there is a negative cost associated with parents spending too much time on devices. When I talk to other parents, read the latest studies, and reflect on my own personal experience, it is increasingly apparent that we have fallen prey to the endless cycle of checking social media, zoning out, and watching reels, and we lack the ability to stay truly present in our homes.

It's fascinating to me how so much attention is placed on children's screen time usage, when many of the parents are using screens just as much (if not more) than their kids. Perhaps that is why we are so concerned about our children using devices? Subconsciously we know we struggle with our own screen addictions, and we are trying to protect our children from the same fate.

If, after this chapter, you would like to make changes to your own screen-time usage, I suggest you use the same tools that you will be teaching your child. It can be really empowering for your whole family when both parents and child commit to changing their behaviors toward screens together.

# TOOL #3: AWARENESS OF YOUR ACTIONS

As I reflect on my own life as a parent during this digital age, I wonder how many moments I have missed with my children because I was too distracted to give them my full attention. I am fully aware of the unhealthy habits that I have developed regarding my phone. Here is just one of them (maybe you can relate?):

Going to my smart phone in moments of annoyance. This action takes the edge off (for a moment) when it comes to the feelings and frustrations I am having with my child.

It doesn't solve the underlying problem that was occurring in the first place however, so when I am more depleted from going into the digital vortex, I emerge less recharged and more reactive.

In a study published in the journal *Pediatric Research*, it was reported that "when parents are on their devices, research shows that they have fewer conversations with their children and are more hostile when their offspring try to get their attention."[22]

If I truly need a break from my children because of overwhelm and I can't use my other tools with them in the moment, then a healthier choice would be to step away and do something restorative (take a walk, take deep breaths, or splash cold water on my hands to bring my awareness back to my senses).

*In the space below, write about times when you notice you are using devices as a way to escape. Do you see a pattern? What could you do differently from now on?*

_____

_____

_____

_____

# TOOL #4: HEALTHY WAYS TO INCREASE DOPAMINE

Let's face it: Life with children can sometimes feel boring and exhausting. We love our kids, but being a present parent can be pretty tough (and sometimes, really, really tough!).

In those tough and/or boring parenting moments, the dopamine of social media can seem like the perfect fix.

Dopamine is a type of neurotransmitter in our brains. It plays a role in how we feel pleasure. Dopamine can be released through food, sex, shopping, social interactions, and more. Much research has been done about the dopamine response a person experiences when on social media. In a talk given by Chamath Palihapitiya, former vice president of user growth at Facebook, Palihapitiya said, "The short-term, dopamine-driven feedback loops that we have created are destroying how society works …"

Palihapitiya goes on to share about the addictive nature of social media.[23]

In another report, Kathryn Lorenz, MD, says that "Prolonged use of watching TV, video games, scrolling through social media—all of that use acts like a digital drug for our brain."

Lorenz goes on to add that "studies have shown screen time affects the frontal cortex of the brain, similar to the effect of cocaine."[24]

Despite a growing awareness around the addictive and unhealthy habits that result from social media, plenty of parents are still using these platforms. And, it is important to add, using them as a way to escape the overwhelm of parenting.

This impacts our children in many ways: not being present, setting an example for overuse of screen time, missing cues our children may be subtly displaying because we are looking down at our phones, failing to meet the physical and emotional needs that our children may have because we are distracted, irritated, and sad from what we view on social media, and suffering the dopamine letdown after we click off.

I feel like that is a good start to a longer list. And I imagine that you have your own experience with going onto social media when your children are home. In the space below, I want to invite you to write down your own experience in this area. Jot down any feelings you had during times you were on social media instead of being present with your child. Of course, it is not always all doom and gloom. This practice isn't about berating social media or yourself.

The writing exercise is to bring awareness of your actions/behaviors with social media *within* your family.

*Which actions/behaviors do you want to change around screen time? What isn't working anymore? When do your behaviors lead you to being a more reactive parent?*

_____

_____

_____

_____

_____

Now that you are clear on what habit you want to change, let's look at healthier actions to help release dopamine in the brain that will nurture your body and help you show up with a full cup to your children.

Healthy dopamine-boosting activities:

» Exercising

» Listening to music

» Getting a good sleep

» Eating healthy foods

» Getting some sunshine and extra vitamin D

» Meditating

» Taking an ice bath or a cold shower (this can be a fun way to increase dopamine; simply try a thirty-second to two-minute cold shower if you aren't ready for the ice)

» Calling a friend

» Getting a massage (you don't have to go to a fancy spa, either. Just rub your feet or give your legs some nice squeezes)

» Bathing in Epsom salt baths

The next time you want to escape on your phone, ask yourself what the best choice is for your overall well-being. Maybe, at that moment, it will be chatting with someone on social media, and that is okay. Just let it be a choice that you make rather than the mind looking for a way to disengage from reality or get more dopamine from an unhealthy source.

# TOOL #5: BEWARE OF THE COMPARE-AND-DESPAIR TRAP

As you scroll through Instagram, Pinterest, TikTok, Facebook, or any of the other social media platforms that I probably am totally unaware of at this point in my life (ha!), you may notice the beautiful homes, manicured gardens, seasonal outfits, and seemingly well-behaved children. Granted, I do have a few friends who will post their child crying on Santa's lap or share the challenges of parenthood, but mostly what I see is a whole bunch of people who look like they have their act together more than I do.

This process of looking at others' exterior lives and then making assumptions about how you don't measure up is what I call the compare-and-despair trap.

First, we compare ourselves to what we see (almost forgetting that we are only seeing what others want us to see), then we compare those beautiful images to the overwhelm and difficulty we are experiencing with our children. The result? A head spinning with worry and old stories of unworthiness.

This emotional roller-coaster doesn't just hurt us. It hurts our children as well. I can remember seeing my friend's children in what I felt was the most perfect photo—they were smiling, were holding hands, and had just gotten out of their gorgeous pool. The filter of the photo had added a sparkly hue to the whole image. Right after viewing that image, my own two children got into an argument. My initial reaction was anger. Anger that there were these two *other* kids with perfect manners (who probably never fought), and my house was a mess, my kids were not behaving, and I felt like a total *failure*.

I had fallen into the trap. I took social media for reality, and we can never truly know what any child's behavior is like when the camera is put away.

*If you find yourself falling into similar traps, I encourage you to take a deep dive into this question: Why do you use social media?*

_____

_____

Whatever your answer to this question, you can create a plan so that you use it as intended (and not as a crutch).

For example, I used social media for a long time when I was first building my parenting business. However, after a while, it became obvious to me that having social media in my life was personally unhealthy. I then proceeded to delete some of my social media accounts and stayed off social media for a period of time. Yet, I came to a tough spot without social media in my career path. So much of my work depends on sharing tools and resources with parents. I do this because I love sharing free resources, and I also do it because in order to get my work to a larger audience, I have to come to terms with the fact that most of those parents are on social media.

After much meditation and reflection, I decided to reengage with social media but with very clear goals—to offer educational support to families and to connect with a few close friends that use social media as their primary form of communication.

Once my mission around social media was clear, I could set myself up with better boundaries. For example, I was able to stop following accounts that were distracting and made my unworthiness flare. I also made sure that my posts were aligned with the mission of teaching parents and children.

By reevaluating my relationship with social media, I was able to take charge of how much time and what kind of time I wanted to spend on any given platform.

I encourage you to do this too!

My hope is that by this point in the chapter, you have some insight into your habits, patterns, and behaviors when it comes to devices. As you start to expand upon your own awareness, you will have the opportunity and gift of setting the tone in your home. You will be able to lead by example when it comes to screen usage, and that is very powerful for our children. As I have said many times in this book but believe is always worth mentioning again: *the parents set the tone of the home!*

Before you can examine the role of screen time with your children, you have to first look at your own relationship with devices. It may not be easy to do, and breaking old habits can be hard. Go easy on yourself, but do notice when a device is pulling you away from your family or trying to fill an emotional void that you have a healthier tool for now.

*Take charge of your devices instead of allowing them to take charge of you!*

As you look at your own relationship with screen time, you might be wondering how to best support your child with their screen-time interactions.

Without further ado, I cover the moment that parents are always asking me about next.

# TOOL #6: SCREEN TIME FOR KIDS!

Or should I call it Scream Time for Kids? I have yet to meet a parent for whom screen time doesn't bring out lots of reactivity.

In structuring this portion of the chapter, I kept thinking about how to make it the most beneficial for you. I decided to include the most frequently asked questions that I get from parents in my workshops, on the playground, during pick-up and drop-off times, at birthday parties, and anywhere I go when someone finds out what I do for a living. These are also the questions asked during any given radio interview and in larger interviews for NBC's *Today Show*, ABC News, and more.

When you read these questions and my answers, I hope that you will keep your family in mind. You know the temperament and needs of your particular child. You also know where you are in your parenting journey. If you have established a routine in your home around screens and want to decrease your family's amount of screen time after reading this book, I would suggest doing so in a way that won't put too much strain on your family too fast. Remember, this book is all about decreasing reactivity in your home and finding more balance and calm. Be gentle as you implement changes.

## SCREEN TIME QUESTIONS

### 1. How much screen time is too much screen time?

Prior to the worldwide shutdown, there had been much concern about screen time and social media use for children and teens. Already, experts were weighing in and parents were trying to find a healthy balance.

Then, as many of us experienced in the COVID-19 pandemic, the use of screen time skyrocketed due to online school for children and parents feeling they needed to use more screens to occupy their children while they were trying to balance working remotely from home.

With the increase of screen time, the fears about usage in children greatly increased. And rightfully so!

With increased use of screens, children get less physical activity and outdoor time. Children are also at increased risk for physical and behavioral concerns, such as "physical health symptoms like eye strain, sleep disturbance, carpal tunnel syndrome, neck pain as well as mental health problems ranging from difficulties in concentration, obsession to diagnosable mental illness, such as anxiety, depression, and attention-deficit hyperactivity disorder."[25]

Of course, much of that added need/want for screens is being reduced as children enter back into classrooms and parents are able to stop playing teacher and show up for their jobs and parenting responsibilities in a more balanced way.

The problem, however, is that many children and teens have become accustomed to their iPads, connecting with friends online and playing video games.

» Children start using digital media devices early in life, with US data suggesting a 32 percent increase in children's screen time over the last two decades.[26]

» COVID screen-time statistics point out that teenagers now spend almost eight hours in front of the screen, and screen time for school isn't included in that time. According to the UCSF-led researchers, the most common recreational activities are watching or streaming videos, gaming, and watching TV shows.[27]

» In 2020, a study by Instagram found that one-third of teen girls said "Instagram made them feel worse," even though these girls "feel unable to stop themselves" from logging on.[28]

» Increased screen time usage in children is considered to be one of the top three harmful effects from the aftermath of the COVID-19 pandemic.[29]

Even with the mounting evidence that too much screen time is harmful, it is hard for parents to take away the devices that were used as a necessity or coping tool.

If we look at the guidelines from the American Academy of Pediatrics and the World Health Organization, they suggest no screen time at all for children until 18 to 24 months, except for video chatting. For children 2 to 5 years old, both organizations suggest an hour or less of screen time per day.[30]

After five years old, it is hard to find a specific number of hours that is recommended. What is clear, though, is that families should create a screen-time plan that feels reasonable and healthy for their child.

Keep the following questions in mind as you develop such a plan.

» How much outdoor time would you like your child to have each day?

» What type of devices do you feel are appropriate to use during the week? In our home, for example, we do allow some age-appropriate video games, but those are only allowed on the weekends. This routine helps us avoid weekday arguments around video games. We will, however, have some television shows during the week when appropriate, but only after other commitments have been completed.

» If you have your own experience with social media, and given what was shared previously in this chapter, how much (if any) social media time are you comfortable with your child using?

» If you are allowing your child to use social media, is it supervised or unsupervised?

» What are your overall family values? If you don't know what your overall family values are (or, if you would like to define them more clearly), this is a good time to create a Family Values Chart. To make a Family Values Chart, sit down and write all of your priorities as a family. What do y'all value most? Let everyone chime in and write all your values down!

Some of the things on our family's list are communication, family activities, playtime with our children, outdoor time, dinners together, quality time, and supporting our children with their homework. After you make your list, you will be able to see where, when, and how often screens make sense for your family.

For example, when we became aware that quality time together was high on our family values chart, then that value began to inform our daily actions.

Will we have our kids sit in front of screens for prolonged periods of time or make space in our schedule for play and connection? The second choice makes more sense when we know what we are trying to accomplish as a family, right?

Copy the Family Values Chart below to get started.

| Family Values |
|---|
| ❏ |
| ❏ |
| ❏ |
| ❏ |
| ❏ |
| ❏ |
| ❏ |
| ❏ |
| ❏ |

## 2. What type of shows are appropriate for your child?

In October 2021 and then again in November 2021, I was interviewed by editor Kait Hanson for two separate articles for NBC's *Today Show*. Both of the interviews were focused on educating parents about what their children may or may not be exposed to in the media and online.

The first interview was around the popular Netflix series, *Squid Game*,[31] a show that was created for mature audiences only, but was (and is) being viewed by children.

The show is confusing for many children who do watch it because it takes common childhood games like Red Light, Green Light but adds an element of violence and death to each game. The result? Children are not always able to differentiate fact from fiction in the way parents may assume.

There have been reports of children acting out the games seen in the show on school playgrounds. One school in Belgium reported some children beat their classmates up after eliminating them.[32]

Whether or not you are allowing your child to watch *Squid Game*, the interview highlights a bigger issue that all of us parents face: *What shows are appropriate, and how do we know?*

One of the biggest problems I see around this for parents is that once several children in a group are allowed to watch something, it becomes normalized within the community.

I personally experienced that with the *Squid Game* when my son quickly began learning about it from friends and then saw kids dressed up as characters from the show on Halloween. He also reported that several of his classmates were watching the show.

If I hadn't just done an interview on the show, I may not have realized the extent of violence depicted in each episode. I may have assumed that because other children his age were allowed to watch the show, it was therefore appropriate for him as well.

This is where it becomes critical that you, as the parent, watch the shows and/or read about the suggested viewing age (and why!) before you allow your child to watch something unattended.

Because the appropriateness of a show, video game, or social media platform is so dependent on your family's values and the maturity of your child, I always encourage parents to take the time to watch what your child is watching. Even though that can feel hard sometimes because their device time is often our babysitter time or break, it really is so important to take a vested interest in what your child is being exposed to. My second interview for *The Today Show* highlights this perfectly.

In November 2021, I was interviewed about an online site called Omegle.[33]

Omegle is a video-chatting site that allows users to connect with strangers. The site can be used to chat using text or video.

Omegle states that users of the site must be eighteen or older to use the site, or thirteen with parental permission and supervision.

What I found from my research is that many times, teens use the site unsupervised and there have been reports of children using the site who were under thirteen years old.

Omegle has been under scrutiny for some time now for its sexual content, predators that have been known to use the site, lack of moderation, and personal security/safety concerns.

And, yet, despite these concerns, Omegle has grown in popularity. According to a *Parents* article by Nicole Harris, this is because TikTok influencers often connect with their fans on Omegle and share their experiences. Children also tend to use Omegle at sleepovers or in other group settings.[34]

When we hear of sites like this being used by children, we must ask ourselves why! Why are children being allowed to use this type of website? Why are parents unaware of the safety concerns associated with the content that their children are exposed to in this digital age?

In my experience, the answer to these questions often comes back to a lack of knowledge on behalf of the parents.

As I previously stated, many parents don't have the time, energy, or interest to watch what their children and teens are watching. And, although this makes sense, I would make a strong case that in this time, when so much is possible for kids to see, it is up to us adults to supervise our children online.

I encourage all parents to really observe and engage with what their children are watching, reading, and listening to. Take the time to read about it on resources like Common Sense Media (https://www.commonsensemedia.org), where you can get reviews from professionals, parents, and children.

Become curious about what your child is watching/doing online and then make guidelines based on your family values.

As you are working toward building a home that is calmer and less reactive, it is important to create an element of safety and protection around screen time.

## 3. What are the effects of social media on children?

We have touched on social media throughout this chapter, but it is worth taking a bit more time to see how social media platforms are affecting our children. When I say children, I am referring to teenagers as well.

In recent news, an ex-Facebook manager, Frances Haugen, criticized the company and said that "Facebook's products harm children, stoke division, and weaken our democracy."

Haugen went on to say that "the company's leadership knows how to make Facebook and Instagram safer but won't make the necessary changes because they have put their astronomical profits before people."[35] Haugen is not the first employee of these larger social media companies to resign and speak out against companies for the addictive and unethical nature of their platforms. The documentary *The Social Dilemma* focuses on the mental health dilemma, the democracy dilemma, and the discrimination dilemma of social media.

TheSocialDilemma.com quotes from the *American Journal of Epidemiology* that "a 5,000-person study found that higher social media use correlated with self-reported declines in mental and physical health and life satisfaction."

In children and teenagers, we see that same compare-and-despair trap I spoke of earlier—comparing internal feelings to the external feelings they perceive others have on social media.

We hear stories of teens wanting to get cosmetic surgery to look the way the filters make them look on Instagram. We hear even more devastating talk of the bullying that happens behind screens that many parents are completely unaware of and don't know is happening to their own child.

In truth, it is a tricky issue to navigate for parents, because when a child's peers are all participating, then the lack of participation brings up feelings of being left out and excluded from the pack.

As each family navigates this for themselves and with their children, the best tools of support are supervision, questions, moderation, and family rules!

## 4. How do screens affect the parent-child relationship?

In the beginning of this chapter, I shared the struggles parents face to connect with their child when devices are pulling them in for work and social connection. I spoke of the negative cycles families can get into when it comes to screens, and you reflected on the habits you would like to create moving forward.

When children are ignored and dismissed due to an overuse of screens, it sends messages to the child about their unworthiness and creates an opportunity for low self-worth to grow.

Of course, this isn't the intention of any parent, but it can be a result of looking down instead of looking into the eyes of your child.

Consider the familiar saying that "the days are long, but the years are short." This window of our children wanting to play with us is not as long as it feels sometimes.

The more connected you are with your child, the less reactive they are (and the less reactive you will be). So often, children misbehave because they do not feel heard, seen, or validated, or because they do not know what the family's routines and limits are. Let's really tune in to our child and tune down the devices. Once you begin on

**BREAK FREE FROM REACTIVE PARENTING**

that path, I am sure you will find your home calming down more than you would have even thought possible.

## 5. How can your family create a balance and a routine around screens?

At the end of the day, it all comes down to balance and routines. Screens are everywhere, and unless you belong to a school community where there is a group agreement of no screens (many Waldorf schools are an example of this) or you homeschool your child, then chances are your child uses screens as a way of connecting socially (and I don't mean social media here). What I mean is that kids talk about their favorite shows, they want to tell each other about the latest video game, and they find connection through those conversations.

Since most of us can't bury our kids' heads in the sand and keep them naive to the world of devices (believe me, I've tried. . .), then we must find a balance within the home that works for us and our children as well.

There are several video games that my son's friends are allowed to play and he is not. Sometimes, that can feel really disappointing to him, but we are always very communicative about our family values, and he understands the choices we make within our home.

With that said, if he goes to a friend's house and they are playing a video game that isn't too inappropriate, I will allow my son to play with them. For us, this is an example of balance. Saying "no" all the time can cause rebellion and frustration. Similarly, we have some games that are reserved for long car rides and airplane trips. Again, this allows for more give and take instead of rigidity.

When we bring flexibility into our homes around screens, coupling that with family agreements, a grasp on what our children are being exposed to, and appropriate monitoring and established routines, the scream time settles down and goes back to screen time.

When putting routines in place, go back to your family values chart. Knowing what you value and what you wish to prioritize as a family will bring more balance to your home because those values can act as your compass when you are deciding how to schedule your days and how/when screens are best used. Because we value family dinners, doing homework together with our kids, after-school activities, and time to play at home, screen time during the week is often not an option because it would require us to take away some of those goals. Thus, the routine of no devices or video games during the week was born to align with what our family values most.

# TOOL #7: SCREEN-TIME TOOL REVIEW

I created a checklist below of all the tools discussed in this chapter so that you can come back and refer to them anytime you need a quick refresher!

» Review content ahead of time with reputable sources such as Common Sense Media.

» Watch and engage in screen time with your child.

» Be present when your child is online.

» Create a family values chart and use that as a guide for developing screen-time rules in your home.

» Tune out of devices and tune in to your child more.

» Be flexible so that your child feels validated in their desires for entertainment, but also remain clear about your family rules (see where you can give to your child while still holding your boundary).

» Look for healthy ways to release dopamine.

» When you are overwhelmed with your child and need a break, use some of the tools in this book (for example, Calming Cards for Kids) to reconnect, and then take a moment for yourself to meditate, journal, go on a walk, or any other calming tool.

In closing, children are often told "no!" around screens without really understanding why. To make matters more confusing, kids are often told "no!" only later to be *allowed* to watch the show or play the video game in a decision that can feel irrational.

As discussed, the reason it so often plays out this way is that parents aren't clear in their intentions around screens or what is appropriate (or at least, you may not have been until reading this chapter). Without that clarity, parents change their minds day to day without conversation around the family values and screen rules.

Once you gain more clarity around screens, you will be able to dive into explaining to children the facts about devices and how they can make better choices that are good for their growing minds and bodies.

As children (and parents!) play a more active and educated role in their device habits, you will breathe a sigh of relief for the calmness that will become created around this very charged subject.

The rest of this chapter will be written for you to read with/to your child.

# FOR YOUR KIDS

**Dear Friends,**

This whole chapter is all about television, movies, iPads, cell phones, and video games. This is a subject I imagine many of you know a lot about and some of you might have big feelings about too!

Some kids really wish their parents would let them watch the same shows that their friends get to watch. Some kids wish that they could play video games. Other kids are allowed to play some video games, but not all the ones that they want to play.

I know kids who wish they could watch shows during dinner. And kids who wish they had family dinners but instead eat every meal in front of the television. As many families as there are in the world, there are tons of different rules about what kids can watch in their home. No single rule works for every family!

Below are some tools that will help you learn about your family's screen-time rules. After learning about them, you may want to make some changes to what you do on screens and how often you use them.

# TOOL #1: IMAGINE YOU WERE THE ADULT

For a moment, I want you to imagine you were a grown-up and had kids of your own. In the spaces below, reflect on each of these questions. You can write the answers yourself or ask your grown-up to help you.

*What shows would you let your children watch?*

_____

_____

_____

*Why would you let them watch those shows?*

_____

_____

_____

*Would you let your child have their own phone?*

_____

_____

_____

*What about a television in their room?*

_____

_____

_____

*What do you wish your family rules were around screens?*

_____

_____

_____

*How do you feel after watching a show or playing video games?*

_____

_____

_____

Sometimes, even if we can't do exactly what we want, it helps to imagine it in our minds. It also helps to think about why your parents have the rules that they do around screens. Have you ever asked them about it? If not, why don't you pause reading and ask them now!

The most important jobs that a parent has are to keep your body and mind healthy, show you love, and keep you safe.

# TOOL #2: POSITIVES AND NEGATIVES OF SCREEN TIME

Over many, many years, people have studied what too much screen time does to growing bodies and brains like yours. It is not all bad, but most of it is not good.

For example, if you are watching screens too often, then you may not go play outside as much. Or you might not get to make up some really cool imaginary games in your room. Also, you may not have as much time to play with your grown-up or sibling, and that is a really special and important time.

It is important to understand what is good and not so good about screens.

In the space below or on a separate sheet of paper, write a list with your parent of the positives and negatives of screen time. Your grown-up can help you with ideas because they just learned a lot in the first part of this chapter!

| Screen-Time Positives | Screen-Time Negatives |
|---|---|
|  |  |
|  |  |
|  |  |

| Screen-Time Positives | Screen-Time Negatives |
|---|---|
| | |

After making your list, do you understand the rules of your home around screens? Do you and your parent think that some new agreements about screens should be made? Now is a good time to do that.

## SCREEN-TIME HOUSE RULES

1. _____

2. _____

3. _____

4. _____

5. _____

What I have found as a teacher and a mom is that sometimes I make rules with my class or my kids, but they are hard to follow (or even remember). Sometimes it helps to write them down and post them to help us remember them!

# TOOL #3: FOUR TIPS TO BALANCE SCREEN TIME

Here are a few tips you can use to help you keep a healthy balance of screen time:

**Use a timer.** Get a kitchen timer and set it for however long you are allowed to watch television, use the iPad, or play a video game that day. If you are allowed to have twenty minutes of screen time, then set the timer for twenty minutes and turn it off when the timer goes off.

**Watch new shows with your parents.** When you are watching a new show for the first time or going online, have a parent sit with you and check it out. This is a great way for both you and your parent to make sure that what you are watching is a good choice (and it is fun to have your grown-up watch with you!).

**Explore screen-free options first.** Before you go on a screen, see if there is something you can play with in your house. Do you have a favorite toy? Or maybe you really like to draw. Or maybe you aren't sure what you like to do yet, and this is a good time to try some new things. Have screen time be a bonus later in the day instead of being something you do all the time or right when you finally have a moment to chill.

**Try something new.** Sometimes kids want to use screens because they are bored! Instead of using a screen the next time you are bored, I want to invite you to try something new. Make a list in the space below of things you like to do when you are bored. My daughter's list includes playing with stuffed animals, drawing, using kinetic sand, painting, coloring by numbers, and building fairy houses. There are so many neat things to do, and being bored is the perfect time to do lots of things on her list. What will you write on your list?

_____

_____

_____

I know that when it comes to screens, parents and kids can have really different ideas of what everyone should be allowed to watch. I understand how frustrating that can feel sometimes.

As your parents discover the best rules for your home, I hope you will join them in bigger conversations about screen time. I hope that you will enjoy your screen time but also enjoy all the other activities available to you each and every day.

Great job in this chapter! You are doing such good work in this book.

With love,

Laura

# CHAPTER 6

# IT'S ALL NEGATIVE SELF-TALK

We have established that today's parents are stressed out, exhausted, and trying to juggle more balls than most of us can keep in the air. With the piling stress and the guilt of feeling like we just aren't doing it right comes the voice of the negative mind. The problem with negative self-talk is that it tends to breed more negativity! And the more negative our state of mind is, the more overwhelming parenting becomes. Additionally, the way that we internally talk to ourselves will often be the external voice we use when we are upset with our children.

Negative self-talk can have different voices. It can be more subtle—*I am not very good at painting, so I might as well not try.* It can appear to be grounded—*I never got good grades in high school and college, so I am not going to go back for another degree because I don't want to do poorly again.* It can be fearful—*Everyone else must be a better parent than I am because their kids all seem like better listeners than mine.* Negative self-talk can be downright mean—*I am not good at anything, and I hate myself for that.*

Whatever form negative self-talk takes in your brain (maybe a combination of several or all the voices, depending on your stress level and mood), it is painful to view your inner and outer world through a lens of a glass being half empty rather than half full. It is painful to talk to yourself in a way that brings you down instead of lifting you up. It is painful to sit with a pessimistic view when there is so much good to see in yourself and in your children.

This chapter, therefore, is devoted to changing the deeply embedded grooves of negative self-talk in the brain so that you can be a *glass half full* kind of guy or gal! We must do everything we can to combat the anxieties and stresses of today's world if we are going to show up as the parents we want to be!

In the words of Daniel J. Siegel from his book *The Whole-Brain Child*, "As parents become more aware and emotionally healthy, their children reap the rewards and move toward health as well. That means that integrating and cultivating your own brain is one of the most loving and generous gifts you can give your children."

With the right tools, hard times become opportunities to build our toolbox so that when life crumbles (and life has a way of doing that), we can stand tall with optimism.

Below, I will share tools rooted in research that I have found personally to be very effective for the negative-thinking mind.

Before I share these tools, however, it is important to note that practicing positive self-talk doesn't mean we minimize our feelings or the feelings of others. I have personally faced many hardships myself and navigated the health crisis of my daughter.

During her scary and uncertain mold fiasco, I was able to maintain the positive outlook that her pain was an opportunity for her to learn more tools around fearful thinking. I knew in my heart that she would emerge with strength from that experience. I helped her to see the positive in the difficult. But that didn't mean that there weren't many soul-aching nights for me. I grieved, I pleaded with the universe, and I had moments of feeling like fear was going to overtake me. All of these emotions were okay and normal. Positive self-talk doesn't mean masking pain but rather being able to be compassionate internally and externally during whatever difficulties we face.

For all parents, this ability to detach from negative self-talk is a must (because, let's face it, the challenges of raising kids makes the happiest of us feel like the pits sometimes).

# TOOL #1: CONTRARY THOUGHTS

Have you ever heard the saying "Act your way into right thinking!"?

I think we could also add to that saying: "Think your way into right thinking!"

Using this tool, we can think our way into positive self-talk, and here is how:

**1.** In the space below, make a list of the common negative things you say to yourself each day. You can make this list in two ways, depending on how aware you are of the inner critic in your head.

**Option A:** If you are very aware of what that negative voice says to you, take some time right now to jot down all the unkind things you catch yourself saying inside your mind.

**Option B:** If you aren't sure exactly what negative self-talk patterns are coming up for you, mark this page with a sticky note and keep a running list over the next week of what you notice.

*Everyday Negative Self-Talk*

_____

_____

_____

_____

_____

Remember, we think six thousand to sixty thousand thoughts each day, and many of those thoughts are negative, repetitive, and rooted in future worries and past regrets.

**2.** As you make this list, you might start to notice an underlying pattern for your negative self-talk. My negative voice when I was ill for so many years was one of being different and not as good as others who were healthy, happy, and smart.

Write down any patterns you notice here.

*Negative Self-Talk Patterns*

_____

_____

_____

_____

_____

**3.** Once you have made your list, use the chart on page 127 to write down five to ten negative self-talk phrases that you would like to change on the left-hand side of the page.

On the right-hand side of the chart, across from each negative phrase, write something positive that you could say as a counter statement.

Here are a few examples:

| Negative Self-Talk | Positive Self-Talk |
| --- | --- |
| I am a bad parent. | I am trying my best as a parent, and I am grateful for my children. |
| I am so dumb. | I feel frustrated when I don't get things right away. But I am willing to learn. What have I done a good job learning in the past? |
| I am ugly. | As I stand in the mirror and look at my body, I can see these five things that I like about myself. |
| I could never learn the parenting tools in this book. I am just not patient enough and my kids are too wild. | I will try a few tools at a time and know that it takes time for kids to learn new habits. I am proud of myself for trying. |

| Negative Self-Talk | Positive Self-Talk |
|---|---|
| | |
| | |
| | |
| | |
| | |
| | |
| | |
| | |
| | |
| | |

**5.** Take a picture of your list and keep it on your phone or print a copy of your list from the book. Keep the list around so that you can refer to it when you notice negative self-talk.

Congratulations! You are on the path to making amazing changes in your life. These may seem like simple exercises, but they produce profound results.

# TOOL #2: ONE KIND ACT EACH DAY

So now that we have coined the phrase "Think your way into right thinking!" let's go back to the more well-known expression "Act your way into right thinking!"

Humans are amazing mammals because we have the ability to reflect on our actions. When we perform a kind act, we can reflect on how that kindness made the other person feel. In turn, thinking about the happiness of another will boost our own mood as well.

As we continue to act in kind ways, our brain takes note of the positive ways we are contributing to the world around us, and that creates more opportunities for positive self-talk.

Although I have always dreamed of being able to volunteer my time fostering children or going into more schools to teach mindfulness and meditation, I have limited ability to do those things at this point in my life. Although those are future goals I have, I can make smaller kind choices each day that add up to making meaningful change.

In his book *Atomic Habits*, James Clear writes, "Every action you take is a vote for the type of person you wish to become. No single instance will transform your beliefs, but as the votes build up, so does the evidence of your new identity."

With this tool, we are taking small actions toward the person we want to become—a person that does good things but also thinks good thoughts about oneself.

I have found that when I am setting a goal like this one, it is not sufficient to simply say that I will do a kind action each day. I might keep the momentum for a day or two, but quickly life will get busy, and my resolution will be forgotten. My trick for staying consistent is creating a chart so I can track my new habits until they become as natural as brushing my teeth every morning and every evening.

Using the chart below as a template, write the date each day and record the kind act you performed. Don't worry about the kind acts being grand or overly complicated. Keep this simple, and as you go throughout each day, notice opportunities for extra kindness.

A few examples from my own life have been sending an email to an author after I finished their book to share what I loved about their story, leaving an anonymous note for someone wishing them a day of happiness, spending extra time playing a game with my children because I know how happy it makes them, leaving a note for my husband under his pillow for him to discover right before bed, and sending groceries to my grandmother in the mail during the pandemic.

What kind acts can you think of? Record them in the chart below and notice if these kind actions have a positive effect on your internal self-talk.

| Date | Kind Act |
|---|---|
|  |  |
|  |  |
|  |  |
|  |  |
|  |  |

# TOOL #3: DAILY JOURNAL PROMPTS

Much of our work in this book has been looking at brain patterns that no longer serve us. When I talk about this process with children, I call it "making a new memory."

For example, when my daughter was scared to ride her bike, I explained that she had the power to make a new memory around that fear by trying her bike on a flat path while I held onto the back. This action, of course, gave her confidence in her ability to ride her bike, and she set out to try again the next day. Little by little, we made new memories until riding a bike went from being scary to being an activity she couldn't wait to do every chance she got.

My son, similarly, made a new memory when he was younger around going to sleep. He went through a phase of having nightmares, and when he was five, I taught him how his dreams were like television shows, and when he woke up from a nightmare, he had the power to switch the channel to a new show. This idea empowered him, and he slowly began to make a new memory around sleep being safe rather than scary.

As adults, we can make new memories too. And we can especially make new memories around negative self-talk. We don't have to continue the cycle of unhelpful feedback we have been telling ourselves for too long now.

The daily journal prompt on the next page will help you feed the voice of positive self-talk. Use it for as long as you need (and feel free to copy the page or print a pdf from my website).

Date: _____

*List three things that went well today.*

_____

_____

_____

*What was one kind act you did for yourself?*

_____

_____

*What was one kind act you did for someone else?*

_____

_____

*What are three positive things you said to yourself today (or you can say right now)?*

_____

_____

_____

*Daily Reflection: Write one or two sentences about tools you are using in your home and how they are helping you. What progress have you noticed that you are proud of?*

_____

_____

# TOOL #4: FOURTEEN OF MY FAVORITE BOOKS

I *love* reading books, and I especially love reading books that help me grow as a person. When I am learning new tools and incorporating practices to boost my mental and physical well-being, I become very aware of the positive effect it has on my thoughts, my marriage, and my relationship with my children.

Although it is hard to just pick fourteen books, I am sharing the books here that are near and dear to my heart because they helped me learn better ways to appreciate and value myself. That, in turn, helped my brain move from negative self-talk to positive self-talk.

**1.** *Big Magic* by Elizabeth Gilbert

**2.** *Atomic Habits* by James Clear

**3.** *The Untethered Soul* by Michael A. Singer

**4.** *When Things Fall Apart* by Pema Chödrön

**5.** *The Surrender Experiment* by Michael A. Singer

**6.** *A New Earth* by Eckhart Tolle

**7.** *The Seven Spiritual Laws of Success* by Deepak Chopra

**8.** *The Gifts of Imperfection* by Brené Brown

**9.** *The Alchemist* by Paulo Coelho

**10.** *The Four Agreements* by Don Miguel Ruiz

**11.** *Happiness: Essential Mindfulness Practices* by Thich Nhat Hanh

**12.** *Full Catastrophe Living* by Jon Kabat-Zinn

**13.** *Comfortable with Uncertainty* by Pema Chödrön

**14.** *Growing Up Mindful* by Chistopher Willard

# FOR YOUR KIDS

In the community I work in, I have noticed an increase in negative self-talk in children compared to a decade ago, when I first began working as a teacher.

Sometimes the negative self-talk is simpler in nature, such as, "I am so dumb."

Other times, negative self-talk from children can sound unnerving and worrisome: "I am the stupidest kid, I hate myself, and I wish I was never born!"

While negative self-talk can be a normal part of expression, parents can help their children with negative self-talk by helping them reframe and get to the *root* of their feelings. Here, we will teach these same tools to children, plus explore the power of positive self-talk in any situation.

The rest of this chapter will be written for you to read with/to your child.

## Dear Friends,

I want to tell you a story about a child who came to me one day because she had gotten in trouble with her mother.

The girl's mother had asked her to get ready to leave the house, but the girl didn't want to leave because she was having so much fun building a Lego horse stable. Because her mom had to leave the house quickly to get the girl's brother to an appointment, the girl felt rushed.

When the girl felt rushed, her hands got hot and her heart pounded louder in her chest— thump, thump, thump. Her teeth locked together so that her jaw felt tight, and she began to growl at her mom like a bear would do—*grrrrr*!

The girl was so mad that when she finally got in the car, she wouldn't stop getting upset with her mom and saying hurtful things. Her mom said that because the girl wasn't acting nicely, they wouldn't be able to watch the show that the girl had been looking forward to seeing. This made the girl super-duper mad—*GRRRRRR*!

After they got home and the girl wasn't as mad anymore, she began to cry to her mom. She said, "I think I am the *worst* kid in the whole world. I am a bad kid. I hate myself!"

Luckily for this little girl, her mom knew something that this girl didn't. Her mom told her daughter that there is no such thing as a bad kid! And that is true (pinky promise).

There really is no such thing as a bad kid. Sometimes kids make choices that aren't okay or that are upsetting, but that doesn't mean that the kid is bad (it just means that the child has a chance to learn how to do something differently and in a kinder way).

When the girl learned this, she felt much better. In fact, her mom taught her daughter the tools that I am going to teach you today. Just like we don't talk meanly to other people, we don't talk meanly to ourselves. This part of the book is learning to talk nicely to yourself!

# TOOL #1: BE CLEAR WITH YOUR WORDS

"I think I am the *worst* kid in the whole world. I am a bad kid. I hate myself!"

When the girl I told you about said those words, she was talking meanly about herself. The problem with talking meanly about yourself is that it makes you feel even worse, and it starts a bad habit of talking meanly to yourself that can stay with you through your grown-up years. Just like you don't want to chew your fingernails your whole life (that hurts your fingernails and prevents them from growing strong), you don't want to get used to saying mean things about yourself your whole life (that can make your mind sad for way too long).

With this tool, you practice being clear with your words. When you make sure to teach yourself kind talk when you are a kid, you will know how to do it when you are all grown up.

For the girl in the story, what she really meant when she said those mean words was "I am really upset that I don't get to watch my show today. I am worried that my mom thinks I am not good at following the rules. I don't like when I get in trouble and can't do what I want to do."

She also meant "I am angry and sad!"

The next time you notice that you are saying mean things about yourself, I want to invite you to try to be clear about what you really mean.

Because this isn't the easiest thing to learn to do (even grown-ups have a hard time with it), I am including some examples here for you to practice. After you read the negative sentence, write down how you could say that in a clearer way that doesn't hurt your own feelings. If you can't yet write, ask your grown-up to help you.

Here are a few examples:

| Negative Saying | Kinder Words |
|---|---|
| I am so dumb! | I am frustrated about what I did! But I do know that everyone makes mistakes sometimes. |
| I am bad at reading, so I won't try. | I am worried about not reading as well as I want to. I will practice a little every day to get better. |
| I hate the way my hair looks. | As I look in the mirror, I say three kind things about the beautiful person I am: 1, 2, 3. |

Now it is your turn to try. Although you may not have had these thoughts before or even feel this way, this is just a chance to practice using kind words rather than negative ones.

| Negative Saying | Kinder Words |
|---|---|
| I am the worst kid. | |
| I don't want to play sports because I don't think I will be good. | |
| I'm not good at school. | |

Good job practicing! If you notice any negative self-talk that shows up again, you can use the space below to write or draw about it. You are on your way to creating a new habit!

# TOOL #2: DAILY REFLECTION: WHAT DO YOU LIKE ABOUT YOURSELF?

One way that you can start thinking kinder toward yourself and stop the voice of negativity is to practice kind talk each day.

In this tool, take the next week or two to write something you like about yourself on a piece of paper each day. Put the paper in a container in your room and read what you wrote with your grown-up each night before bed.

Do you notice that you like this tool? If you do, keep going! You can keep doing it for as long as you want.

# TOOL #3: WHAT DO YOU DO WHEN YOU MAKE A MISTAKE?

We all make mistakes. This is part of being a human. We get angry and yell, we mess up during a big game, we fall off our bikes, we act too goofy even though we have been told to stop, and we answer a question wrong in school.

It is normal to make mistakes, but sometimes when we make a mistake, we can start to feel bad about ourselves and talk negatively out loud or in our minds.

There is a book about making mistakes that I really like. It is about a person who is drawing a picture and makes a mistake on the drawing. Instead of throwing away the paper, though, the person keeps adding to the picture, and the picture ends up being big and beautiful.

The next time you are at the library or bookstore, ask your grown-up if you can check it out. It is called *The Big Book of Mistakes*, by Corinna Luyken.

I love this book because the artist doesn't give up when they make a mistake. And, at the end of the story, they learn that by making the mistake, there was a chance to learn and to make things better.

That is the takeaway of this tool for your toolbox: *It is okay to make mistakes!*

The next time you make a mistake, see if you can try to be kind to yourself. See if you can notice a chance to learn something. Don't let your mistake make you feel bad!

# TOOL #4: KINDNESS COUNTS: ONE KIND ACT EACH DAY

The last tool for changing negative self-talk into positive self-talk is doing one kind act each day.

Doing kind acts not only makes other people feel better, but also makes you feel better about the person you are!

Every time you do an act of kindness, you make new paths in your brain that show you how special you are in this world.

This tool is a challenge: to do one kind act each day for a month! That might seem like a long time, but I know you can do it.

It's All Negative Self-Talk

In the space below, write down your start date and then each date for the next month. Every day after you have done one kind act, give yourself a check mark.

| Start Date | Kind Act |
|---|---|
| ☐ | |
| ☐ | |
| ☐ | |
| ☐ | |
| ☐ | |
| ☐ | |
| ☐ | |
| ☐ | |
| ☐ | |
| ☐ | |
| ☐ | |
| ☐ | |
| ☐ | |
| ☐ | |
| ☐ | |
| ☐ | |
| ☐ | |
| ☐ | |
| ☐ | |

**BREAK FREE FROM REACTIVE PARENTING**

| Start Date | Kind Act |
|:---:|---|
| ❑ | |
| ❑ | |
| ❑ | |
| ❑ | |
| ❑ | |
| ❑ | |
| ❑ | |
| ❑ | |
| ❑ | |
| ❑ | |
| ❑ | |

Be creative with your kind acts. The person you are doing the kind act for doesn't have to know about it for it to count. For example, you could push in a friend's chair for them in class if they forgot to. Or, if you notice your sibling left their favorite stuffy on the ground, you could put it on their bed for them.

I can't wait for you to come up with your own ideas of kind acts! And friends, you are doing such good work in this book. Your toolbox is getting really big now, and I am so proud of you for continuing to do the activities for this chapter and throughout the book.

With love,

Laura

# CHAPTER 7

# DID YOU HEAR WHAT I SAID?

Do you feel like your children have selective hearing? Are you asking them five billion times to do something before they respond with a grunt, a groan, or potentially a flat out "No!"? Are you pretty sure every other kid seems to listen better than your own?

When I hold a workshop for parents, I often begin by asking parents to call out all the things that are driving them nuts about their children and what they hope they can change. One of the first responses is always someone yelling out, "My kids won't listen!" At that point, a sea of heads all start nodding in agreement.

Here's the truth: Our kids aren't here to listen to our every command! And yet, with that said, children not listening is a universal problem, which requires some education for parents and practical tools for engaging our children more and ordering them around less.

The good news is you are not alone in the "kid not listening" department. For me, not being heard is an old wound that I have carried with me. I have often felt unheard, and therefore, when my children don't listen to me, it brings up those really strong feelings of anger, sadness, and low self-worth.

Parenting is like this in many ways. When we have a big reaction to a behavior that our children are doing, it is an opportunity to look into our past.

In the book *The Conscious Parent*, Shefali Tsabary writes about the importance of consciousness for parents so that we are better able to tune in to our children and stop the family cycle of pain. Tsabary says, "Our children pay a heavy price when we lack consciousness. Overindulged, over-medicated, and over-labeled, many of them are unhappy. This is because, coming from unconsciousness ourselves, we bequeath to them our own unresolved needs, unmet expectations, and frustrated dreams. . .only through awareness can the cycle of pain that swirls in families end."

When I don't feel heard, a cycle starts with my children when they don't listen: I react, they listen less because I am in reaction, and I react more. As long as I am unconscious of this pattern of behavior, I stay stuck in this cycle.

The hope is written in Tsabary's last line, "only through awareness can the cycle of pain that swirls in families end."

So, I do my own work first. I look at the pain that not being heard brings up in me historically and in the present. I cultivate tools for when these deep-seated feelings arise (you have learned many already in this book, and you will learn more specific tools in Section II). I shine the light of awareness on the feelings that arise in my body when I ask one of my children to listen (and then have to ask again and again).

It is after I do the internal work on myself and I begin to shift the old narrative of equating not being heard with not being lovable that I can show up as the mother I want to be when my child doesn't listen.

Because so many parents feel quite triggered by their children when they don't listen, part of this chapter is looking at our own personal history. It is only through awareness that the tools can become effective.

Please note that if your child not listening is not something that upsets you, then use Tool #1 for other behaviors that make you want to yell or retreat. We can apply many of the tools in this book to all different kinds of feelings and behaviors, and they will be just as effective and powerful.

# TOOL #1: WHAT'S MY PART? AND CONTRARY ACTIONS!

My two children were wrestling on the couch—one of their favorite games to play—until someone inevitably got hurt. It was time for us to get ready to leave the house, and I asked several times for my children to stop wrestling.

In a loud voice I asked, "Can you hear me?"

With no response and continued wrestling, I got closer and told them both to stop and go sit until they were ready to listen.

My son made a snarky comment, to which I responded, "Please go to your room!"

When I felt calmer, I circled back with my son, only to find that he was continuing to act silly and unconcerned with the choices of his behavior.

I snapped. My anger came out. I was that ten-year-old girl that didn't feel heard. My reaction was disproportionate to the behavior of my son.

I saw where the wounded part of me was acting out. At that moment, I knew I had to go back to our most important parenting tool: self-regulation.

After I was calm again and the kids were calm, I invited them to have a mini family gathering. We started by sharing appreciations for each person in the gathering and followed up by owning our parts in the argument. Then, we talked about how we could handle a situation like that in the future. My daughter reminded me of the special hand signal we created for when I want her to listen to me.

Because I have been working at this for many years, I didn't stay in my lack of awareness for very long. I did, however, stay in it long enough to regret the anger that I displayed toward my kids (especially my son).

In this tool, the game changer is being able to see your own historical triggers *before* reacting to your children. Easier said than done, I know! But also very doable when you have the right tools and motivation for change.

## WHY IT'S IMPORTANT TO PAY ATTENTION TO YOUR BEHAVIORAL PATTERNS

Did you know that you can inherit your parents' (or grandparents'/caretakers') parenting habits without even realizing it? When you're a child, you observe the actions of those around you, and those behaviors can get imprinted into your subconscious mind, creating an autopilot, knee-jerk response to certain situations. For example, if you catch yourself resorting to yelling or punishing your child, look back to your own childhood: Did your parents do the same? Although our parents may have meant well, it doesn't necessarily mean the habits we acquired from our childhood will benefit our own family.

## HOW TO USE THE CREATING NEW BEHAVIORS CHART

The Creating New Behaviors Chart features two columns: Old Behaviors and New Behaviors. Write down old parenting patterns and old beliefs that keep you in a reactive state (e.g., yelling, bribing, not feeling heard) on the left side, then write a new pattern that you would like to implement and develop on the right side. Here are a few examples for your reference:

| Old Behaviors | New Behaviors |
| --- | --- |
| Yelling at my child when they're having a temper tantrum. | When my child is upset, I am going to remain calm and take a few deep breaths before approaching the situation. I am in charge of a solution for both me and my child. |
| Letting my child do as they wish and being passive about my parenting. | Be more proactive about my parenting and resolve the issue with the help of the Calming Cards (see Chapter 2). |

The purpose of this chart is to help you understand your behavioral patterns and be more mindful about your parenting choices. What isn't serving you or your child's overall well-being? What beliefs and habits can be undone and replaced with a new routine that produces more calm and joy in your home? What would you like to change about your parenting or your child's behavior, and what can you do to create those changes?

Take your time with the Creating New Behaviors Chart shown below. Sometimes, self-reflection can be a hard pill to swallow, but I assure you that you will only grow and further develop more conscious parenting decisions after this. Be kind to yourself when you're doing this exercise. You can even take it one behavior at a time and add more new behaviors later on. Download this chart at www.LauraLinnKnight.com/freebies; print as many charts as you wish!

| Old Behaviors | New Behaviors |
|---|---|
| | |
| | |
| | |
| | |
| | |
| | |

# TOOL #2: ORDER LESS, ASK MORE, AND OFFER A CHOICE!

When it comes to children not listening, I have worked with enough parents over the years to understand that not feeling heard by your own child is one of the most frustrating parenting problems we all face.

In the beginning of this book, we saw how self-regulation is the keystone to having a calmer internal state (and thus a calmer home). Awareness of our old patterning and downloads is that next fundamental step toward the healthy family unit we all desire.

With these two crucial skills—self-regulation and awareness—you are now well on your way to making sure the tools you have learned thus far in this book can continue to be effective (remember, these tools are hard to use when in the lower part of our reptilian brain and in a reactive state).

With the understanding and peace that come from self-regulation and awareness, we have the opportunity to tackle the highly triggering (and very common) difficulty of kids not listening.

In Chapter 2, we talked about how often children are told "No!" throughout the day. All those noes can make a child feel frustrated and annoyed. In Tool #3: Order Less and Ask More (page 45), I introduced the tool of making fewer demands on our children and instead being more curious with them.

The premise of this tool is that when we ask a child—instead of telling them—what to do, we invite a level of engagement that we wouldn't otherwise see. This tool is effective for power struggles, and it is also very effective for children not listening (which, of course, goes hand in hand with power struggles).

Dr. Jane Nelsen, founder of Positive Discipline (a parenting program that teaches kind yet firm parenting strategies), writes, "When parents say, 'My child doesn't listen,' what they really mean is that my child doesn't obey. Parents give orders and children resist orders—just as their parents most likely would. . . .Parents do too much 'telling' instead of 'asking,' and then listening. They tell their children what happened, and then tell them what caused it to happen, and then tell them how they should feel about what happened, and then tell them what they should do about what happened. It is much more effective to ask a child what happened, what caused it to happen, how she feels about it, and what she can do about it."[36]

In Dr. Laura Markham's blog, *Aha! Parenting*, there is a wonderful article about how to get your child to listen. It states, "no one wants to listen to someone who's giving orders; in fact, it always stimulates resistance. Think about how you feel when someone orders you around. Do you cooperate enthusiastically? Instead, keep your tone warm. When possible, give choices."[37]

In my own work with children, especially as an elementary school teacher, I saw Dr. Nelsen's and Dr. Markham's powerful points in daily action. One example is of a student who could have easily been labeled "defiant." There was so much work in the classroom that the student didn't want to participate in, and getting this student to follow directions was not an easy task. If I had taken an authoritative role with him, he would have recoiled from my directions and tuned me out. Instead, it was imperative that I invited this student to be an active participant and feel like schoolwork was a choice rather than an order.

What that looked like was being curious with this student. *How can you set aside time to get your math done during this next hour so that you can get back to the book you are reading?* This particular student loved reading! Getting this student to be an active participant looked like asking him to be a helper in the classroom when I could see the wiggles coming out, to think of ideas he could use when he was upset, and to think of ways that he could take a participatory role in class rather being nagged at. When this student was unregulated, I would first connect and then ask questions about how he was feeling and what he was thinking and then help him to problem-solve and create a plan. The result was that this student had a very good school year and grew so much socially and emotionally (as well as academically).

I share this story because it shows the power of curiosity. It is a testimony to children feeling empowered to participate in their school life (and home life!) when they are told less and asked more.

Additionally, another way to encourage your child to listen better (and follow through) is to offer a choice. When you ask your child a question, you automatically get them into their critical-thinking mind. For example, "Go do your homework now" is very different from, "How would you like to begin your homework tonight? Should we start with math or reading?" Just the nature of the choice invites participation.

The next time you are looking for more active engagement from your child in the listening department, try asking a question and/or offering a choice!

# TOOL #3: GETTING DOWN TO EYE LEVEL

Have you ever noticed how when you get louder, your children get louder? The escalating chaos makes parents want to yell "Be quiet!" which often has the opposite effect we were ultimately hoping for (and makes our children want to listen less).

When we want our children to listen, we should think about how we listen best. Take a moment to reflect on the questions below:

*How do you feel heard in a conversation?*

_____

_____

_____

*When was a time that you felt really listened to?*

_____

_____

_____

*When someone wants you to do something, how do you like them to ask you?*

_____

_____

_____

*Think of a time when a friend or a coworker told you to do something in a harsh tone. How did that make you feel?*

_____

_____

_____

Our children deserve to be treated with the same dignity that we would like to be treated with ourselves. I personally don't respond well to yelling, and being ordered around makes me want to recoil as if from a hot flame.

Now, before I go on, I know what many of you may be thinking. I know because I often get this question in parenting workshops: "But my children need to be able to follow directions and do as they are told, right?"

The short answer is yes (but to a certain degree). The longer version of that is we want children who can show respectful behavior in our home. We want children who participate in the daily chores and upkeep of our homes. We want children who hear us and do their best each day to make good choices. But we don't want children who blindly follow orders out of fear. We do not want to raise children who are shamed into listening. Those tools work in the short term, but long-term studies on growing up in those types of home environments show a greater chance of rebellion, addiction, and low self-worth.

When we treat children with respect time and time again, they will treat us respectfully back. When you don't feel heard by your child, you can talk to them the way that you would like to be talked to.

This tool is the physical action of getting down to the eye level of your child (or a little below) and quietly telling them what you need them to do. You may try doing this with the asking tool from pages 45 and 46.

When you set the stage of calm and are considerate in your tone, you will be surprised by how much more cooperative your child will become. Of course, there will be times when you use all the right tools, and your child still won't listen. When that moment happens (and it will!), you can decide what the logical consequence will be for your child. You may also decide to have your child sit for a moment until everyone is calm enough to use this tool (or another tool from the book).

Remember, there is an ebb and flow to life and an ebb and flow to parenting. Not every tool works every time and not every child will respond the same way to each tool. The goal is that we have enough tools and understanding to raise happy, generous, and kind humans.

In her book, *Raising Good Humans*, Hunter Clarke-Fields says it beautifully: "Children tend to be terrible at doing what we say but great at doing what we do."

With this tool, we are modeling respect, curiosity, and calmness as we get low to the ground, lower our voice, and ask for cooperation.

# TOOL #4: CREATE ROUTINES

Throughout this book, we have talked about the benefits of creating routines within the home. Routines create stability and offer structure, which makes children feel safe and takes away a lot of the daily power struggles.

We have already gone over how to establish morning and nighttime routine charts in previous chapters, but are there other areas of your daily life where your child could benefit from a routine?

In our home, I ask my children to help me separate the laundry to fold after it has been washed. They know after each meal to clear their plates and put them next to the sink. We also have the routine of nightly appreciations that we share from our day.

Whatever the routine you are trying to create, take time to introduce it and be patient, as your child will need reminders until the routine becomes a habit. As routines become established, they will clear a space where you find yourself giving directions less often. And when you do need to ask for your child's attention, they will be more open to listening because they haven't been overloaded with directions or orders from the day.

# FOR YOUR KIDS

You have now learned some really powerful tools for helping your child listen more. My hope is that you are feeling empowered to develop routines and use your toolbox around the common times when your children's ears seem to shut off, such as when they are getting ready for school, going through the bedtime routine, turning off a video game, and cleaning up.

For your child, this chapter is now packed full of listening games and creative ways to boost their listening skills.

Children will find the fun in listening and build their listening muscle as you play these family games and do the exercises. I will also share some guided mindful-listening activities that will help create better long-term habits.

This chapter is geared toward finding the fun in listening games/ activities so that listening can be a practiced skill. Listening, as a skill, is not necessarily like the other tools we have shared in this book thus far. Those tools were more concrete (e.g., making a pause poster for times when your child is upset, creating calming down cards, and putting together a kindness box). Listening is different from the emotions that we have been working on because it is a skill, one that needs to be developed over time.

This chapter is geared to help your child develop their listening skills so that the tools you are using in the beginning of the chapter can work more effectively.

The remainder of this chapter will now be written for your child.

**Dear Friends,**

This chapter is about listening. More specifically, listening when grown-ups ask you to do something. Sometimes, we grown-ups wonder if you kids are listening to us or can even hear what we are trying to say!

Sometimes, when my son is building Lego blocks, I will say his name, and then say his name again, and then say his name again. . .Oh, and then I might say his name again! Finally, he'll look up at me and say, "What?"

That kind of not listening comes from him being so interested in an activity that his mind is just thinking of that one thing. Other times, I might ask him to bring in his backpack from the car. He says that he will, but then I need to ask him again and again and again. That kind of not listening can feel frustrating for grown-ups because they have to ask the same thing many times. But it can also feel frustrating for you, as the child, because you are being asked to do the same things over and over again.

In the section above, I wrote about tools that your adults can use to help make listening easier for everyone at home. Now, it is your turn to learn tools that will help you keep your listening ears alert at home (and at school)!

# TOOL #1: LISTENING GAMES

Do you like playing games with your grown-up? My kids love it when we play games together with our whole family or just one on one.

Below, I have included some of my children's favorite games and how to play them. Chances are, you may have played them before! I also left some room at the end of this tool for you to write in some of your favorite listening games, in case you may want to play more.

## LISTENING GAME #1: TELEPHONE

**Number of Players:** Three or more

**How to Play:** Sit in a circle and decide who will go first. The first person begins the game by whispering a sentence into the ear of the person sitting next to them. For example, the sentence might be, "I have a cat. Her name is Boots."

Then, the person who just heard the sentence will turn to the person sitting next to them and try to whisper the sentence just as they heard it. That person will turn to the next person and again try to whisper the sentence just as they heard it.

The goal is to make it all the way around the circle and see if the original sentence that was whispered turns out to sound the same by the time the last person says it out loud for the whole group to hear.

The last time I played this game with my family, we started with the sentence, "I hear the telephone ring" and ended with the last person thinking the sentence was, "I broke the telephone." Fun, right?!

## LISTENING GAME #2: RED LIGHT, GREEN LIGHT

**Number of Players:** Two or more

**How to Play:** Decide who will go first. This person will be the caller, calling "Red Light," "Green Light," or "Yellow Light"! Everyone else will be the players.

Red Light means STOP.

Yellow Light means SLOW DOWN.

Green Light means GO.

Find a starting line for all the players to stand on.

The caller stands away from the players at the place you have determined to be the finish line.

When the caller says "Green Light," everyone will move toward them. When they call out "Yellow Light," the players will slow down. "Red Light" means stop.

If a player moves when the caller says "Red Light," then that player must go back to the starting line.

The goal of the game is to make it to the finish line first.

## LISTENING GAME #3: SIMON SAYS

**Number of Players:** Two or more

**How to Play:** Decide who will go first as the Simon of the game. This person tells the group what to do, but Simon must say "Simon says" before each thing that they say to do.

For example, if Simon wants everyone to tap their heads, they must say, "Simon says, tap your head!"

The players must only do the things that begin with the words "Simon says."

Simon will try to trick the players by sometimes saying "Simon says" and other times just telling them what to do.

For example, Simon may say:

Simon says, tap your head.

Simon says, clap your hands.

Simon says, stick out your tongue.

Touch your toes.

Notice how the last direction didn't have the "Simon says" in front of it. Any player who then touched their toes would be out for that round.

The winner is the person who lasts until the end and doesn't follow a direction that Simon didn't say to do.

After one person is Simon for a round, it is then time to switch.

## LISTENING GAME #4: GUESS THE ANIMAL GAME

**Number of Players:** Two or more

**How to Play:** One person thinks of an animal in their mind (Shhh! Don't say the animal out loud yet.).

The other people playing can ask yes or no questions about what the animal might be. The goal is to guess the animal that the person has thought of.

For example, you might ask questions like:

Does the animal live on land?

Does the animal eat grass?

Have you seen this animal in our neighborhood before?

Have you seen this animal at a zoo before?

Is the animal bigger than a chair at school?

By asking yes or no questions, it will help you figure out what animal the person was thinking of. Afterward, it is someone else's turn to think of an animal.

Do you have other listening games that you love to play? If so, write them in the space below!

_____

_____

_____

# TOOL #2: MINDFUL-LISTENING MEDITATION

Noises are all around us, and sometimes it is neat to see just how far we can stretch our listening to discover the sounds in our home, school, or neighborhood. I like to do this listening meditation in different places to see how the sounds change. At night in my home, I hear cars driving outside and my husband downstairs cleaning up after dinner. During the day, I hear neighbors walking their dogs, delivery trucks, and dogs barking. When we are camping, I hear birds during the day and crickets at night. The sounds change depending on what time of day it is and where I am.

Wherever you are right now, I invite you to find a safe place to sit or lie down and close your eyes (or softly gaze at the ground or ceiling). Take a deep breath into your belly through your nose and let the breath out through your mouth.

Notice as you keep taking breaths the way your tummy goes up and down.

Now, turn your attention to the sounds you can hear from where you are. Perhaps the sounds are loud. Notice how those sounds feel in your body. Maybe it is so quiet that the only noise you really notice is the sound of your breath. Notice how that sound feels in your body.

You can make a list in your mind of the sounds you hear right now. Then, try this listening meditation again another time and see how the sounds are the same and different.

This is a great tool for practicing listening, but it is also one that I use a lot with kids when they are feeling worried. Being aware of the sounds in our space can shift our worrying minds back into the moment.

# TOOL #3: MAKING A RAIN STICK

When I was in third grade, I made my own rain stick at school. I had done lots of art projects before making that rain stick, and I did many projects afterward. But out of everything I ever made at school, the rain stick was my favorite.

I loved listening to the sound of the beans and rice falling down through the maze of nails that I had carefully placed inside the tube (we used nails then, but you can make your rain stick with craft wire or pipe cleaner—more of that to come in a moment). The cardboard tube that I had painted purple made my rain stick feel special and fun. It was a craft that I had with me for many, many years, and it is something that you can make too.

After your rain stick is all done and dry, I invite you to listen to the beans and rice falling through the rain stick just like I used to do.

Do they sound differently when you hold the rain stick to the side?

What kind of sound do you hear if you shake the rain stick?

Does it feel good to listen to the "rain" when you are sad, scared, or mad?

You can also make your rain stick your official family listening tool. When someone needs to get everyone's attention, they can make the rain sound as a cue for everyone to gather quietly around.

Here I am including directions so you and a grown-up can make the rain stick together:

## MATERIALS

- ❑ Cardboard tube (The longer the tube, the more sound you will hear. Also, make sure the cardboard is sturdy; the cardboard tube from inside an aluminum foil roll can be good.)
- ❑ Paint (Tempera paint can be nice and thick for the project.)
- ❑ Scissors
- ❑ Construction paper or a paper bag
- ❑ Rubber bands
- ❑ Craft wire or pipe cleaner
- ❑ Dried beans and/or dried rice

## DIRECTIONS

**1.** Paint the outside of the cardboard tube and let it dry.

**2.** Cut two large circles from the construction paper or the paper bag.

**3.** Rubber band the paper around one end of the tube and make sure it is secure.

**4.** Coil the craft wire or pipe cleaner and place it inside the cardboard tube. This will be what the beans/rice hit against to give it the sound of rain.

**5.** Pour the beans and/or rice into the top of the tube. Be mindful about how much you pour in. If you have too many, then there won't be space to make the sound because they will all get clumped together.

**6.** Seal the top of the tube with the second piece of paper and a rubber band.

**7.** Listen to your rain stick when you turn it upside down!

# TOOL #4: AUDIOBOOKS AND PODCASTS FOR KIDS

Listening to stories is something I love, and it is also one of my son's most favorite things to do.

In our home, we have time to read stories out loud with everyone. But, sometimes, when I am busy or my son wants to hear a book that he can't read yet or he wants some alone time, he will ask to listen to an audiobook.

There are several ways to listen to an audiobook. You can buy CDs or tapes to play in a music player. You can listen on a grown-up's phone if they say it is okay. Or, you can find stories online to listen to (be sure you ask a grown-up to help you find ones that are for your age) or have your grown-up help you find a kid's podcast.

Listening to books on audio can be relaxing because you can imagine the story in your mind, you can learn new words and become a better reader, and it can improve your listening skills. Way cool, right?

Here are a few books that we love to listen to in our home. I divided them by grade level!

**Tip:** If you can't find all these books on audio or you aren't able to buy them, you can check out the books from the local library and then record them on your phone for your child to listen to later. It's also great to peruse podcasts and audiobooks that reflect your child's interests or culture.

## KINDERGARTEN

» *Mercy Watson* by Kate DiCamillo

» *Zoey and Sassafras* by Asia Citro

» *The Frog and Toad* Collection by Arnold Lobel

## FIRST GRADE

» *Nate the Great* by Marjorie Weinman Sharmat

» *Meet Yasmin!* by Saadia Faruqi

- » Magic Tree House series by Mary Pope Osborne
- » *Cam Jansen* by David A. Adler
- » *Jokes for Kids* by Joe Kozlowski
- » *Ada Twist and the Perilous Pants* by Andrea Beaty

## SECOND GRADE

- » *Dory Fantasmagory* by Abby Hanlon
- » *The Mouse and the Motorcycle* by Beverly Cleary
- » *My Father's Dragon* by Ruth Stiles Gannett
- » *Charlie and the Chocolate Factory* by Roald Dahl
- » *Good Night Stories For Rebel Girls* by Elena Favilli and Francesca Cavallo

## THIRD GRADE

- » *Spy School* by Stuart Gibbs
- » *Make Way for Dyamonde Daniel* by Nikki Grimes
- » *Charlotte's Web* by E.B. White
- » *Moon Base Alpha* by Stuart Gibbs

## FOURTH GRADE

- » *Winnie-the-Pooh* by A. A. Milne
- » Alvin Ho series by Lenore Look
- » *Because of Winn-Dixie* by Kate DiCamillo
- » *The Mysterious Benedict Society* by Trenton Lee Stewart
- » *The Wild Robot* by Peter Brown

## FIFTH GRADE

- » *Wonder* by R. J. Palacio
- » *The Chronicles of Narnia* Series by C. S. Lewis

» *The Hobbit* by J. R. R. Tolkien

» *When Stars Are Scattered* by Victoria Jamieson and Omar Mohamed

» *One Crazy Summer* by Ritta Williams-Garcia

# TOOL #5: STORY GAMES

My daughter and I love to play story games. Sometimes, we play by just making up a regular story and sometimes we play with rhyming stories. You can be creative and add to your stories and make new rules as you expand on this fun listening game.

Here are the directions for the original story games we play in our home.

**Number of Players:** Two or more

**How to Play:** One person begins the story with a sentence or two. For example, they might say, "Once upon a time, there was a bunny who was really embarrassed. The bunny was embarrassed because. . ."

Then, the next person picks up the story and continues to tell it with another one or two sentences. For example, "The bunny was embarrassed because instead of eating carrots like all the other bunnies, he only wanted to eat pie."

Now, it is the next person's turn to add onto the story. They might say something like, "The bunny had tried apple pie one day when the farmer's wife had left it out to cool on the windowsill. Now, the bunny thought of pie all day long! He knew he had to make a plan to get more pie. . ."

I bet you get the idea now, right? Each person keeps adding to the story until it becomes complete!

Did you have fun playing that game? If the answer is yes, create a new story and start again.

I hope you will enjoy these listening games and activities as much as we do in our home. They are a great way to practice listening while having a whole lot of fun.

With love,

Laura

# CHAPTER 8

# IT'S TOOL TIME!

You have read, written, drawn, played, joked (and possibly cried) your way through self-regulation, power struggles, sibling fighting, worry, screen time, negative self-talk, and not listening.

You now have a toolbox of life-changing resources that will help shape your future and your family's.

The best way to not give up on your toolbox (and not forget about it) is to review what you have learned and make a copy of the toolbox I am providing on pages 163 and 164 for you and your child to hang in your home and to keep safely somewhere in your car.

This chapter may be brief, but it is mighty in its importance! Nothing changes unless you *use* the tools in the moment! When you're mad, worried, stressed, exhausted, or seeing red. When you could react and instead reach for a tool—that's real change. And it matters.

So, let's make a checklist of our tools for you to keep coming back to. And notice if you find yourself mixing and matching the tools (that is great too).

You may notice that some of the tools for not listening also work well for sibling fighting. The idea is to be fluid and learn to trust your instincts as the amazing, hardworking, and inspiring parent that you are!

Notice that I have the tools in order from each chapter, but I did not label them from each chapter, as I really want to encourage you to see these tools as a giant toolbox you now have to use in a range of different scenarios. Quite honestly, you will be amazed by how these tools will begin to expand and work in all relationships when given a little finesse and twist. They can help with your extended family, partner, and work community.

# TOOLBOX FOR YOU

- ❏ *Self-Regulation for Adults:* Guided Reflections, Plan-to-Pause Poster, Favorite Calming Quotes to Inspire Change, Daily Prompts, and the Dos and Don'ts of Self-Regulation

- ❏ *Power Struggles for Adults:* Calming Cards for You; The 3 P's: Problem-Solve, Plan, Patience; Order Less and Ask More; and Empathy through Storytelling

- ❏ *Sibling Rivalry Tools for Adults:* Fair Treatment, Be Present, Special One-on-One Time, and Play Together as a Family

- ❏ *Tools for the Worrying Mind for Adults:* Dot Activity, Write It Out and Rip It Up, Get to the Root, Positive Affirmations, and Meditation

- ❏ *Screen-Time Tools for Adults:* Reflection Questions, Dopamine Alternatives, Solidifying Overarching Family Goals, and Tips for Creating Balance and Routine

- ❏ *Negative Self-Talk Tools for Adults:* Contrary Thoughts, One Kind Act Each Day, Daily Journal Prompts, and Six of My Favorite Books

- ❏ *Tools to Help Kids Listen for Adults:* What's My Part? and Contrary Actions; Order Less, Ask More (continued from Chapter 2), and Offering a Choice; Getting Down to Eye Level; and Creating Routines

## TOOLS TO COME

- ❏ *Mindfulness Tools for Adults:* Mindful Eating, Mindful Cleaning, Mindful Self-Compassion, Mindful Meditation, Mindful Listening, Mindful Walking

- ❏ *Tools for Your Morning and Nighttime Routine:* Carve Out Time Each Morning for Meditation, Morning Quiet Reflection with Journal Prompt, Morning Gratitude Ritual, Evening Thank-You Box, and Healthy Evening Habits

# TOOLBOX FOR YOUR CHILD

- *Self-Regulation for Kids:* Plan-to-Pause Poster for Kids, Big Belly Breaths, Wonderful Picture Books to Read, Coloring Pages to Help Chill Out

- *Power Struggles for Kids:* Flower Petal Trick, Kids Calming Cards, Mini Gathering, Write or Draw It Out, Offer a Hug or Ask for One

- *Sibling Rivalry Tools for Kids:* Plan Playtime, Create a Project Together, Kindness Box, and Picture Books

- *Tools for the Worrying Mind for Kids:* What Do You See, Hear, Smell, and Feel?; Name the Worry; Big Breaths; Practice and then Practice Again; and Changing the Movie in Your Mind

- *Screen Time Tools for Kids:* The Pros and Cons of Screen Time, Creating Family Screen Time Rules, and Being Bored List

- *Kind Talk for Kids:* Be Clear with Your Words, Daily Reflection: What Do You Like about Yourself?, What Can You Do When You Make a Mistake?, and Kindness Counts: One Kind Act Each Day (How Creative Can You Be?)

- *Tools for Listening for Kids:* Listening Games, Mindful Listening Meditation, Making a Rain Stick, Audio Stories, and Story Games

## TOOLS TO COME

- *Mindfulness Tools for Kids:* Mindful Body Scan, Mindful Eating, Mindful Breath, Mindful Walking, and Meditation

- *Tools for Your Child's Morning and Nighttime Routine:* Morning Gratitude at Breakfast; Three Simple Morning Stretches; Mini Morning Story; Short Morning Meditation; Evening: Rose, Bud, and Thorn; and Evening Thankful Box

# SECTION 2:

# CREATE MEANINGFUL CHANGE

# CHAPTER 9

# MIND-FULL TO MINDFUL

Meditation and mindfulness have become quite the buzz words in the last decade. Some people love the concepts and others retract from them as if they were dirty socks.

Because you have done so much important work in the first section of this book and built your toolbox in a profound way, my hope is that by introducing or building upon an already-existing mindfulness/meditation practice, you will deepen your ability to use your parenting tools.

This is where our work must go next. It is important that you give yourself the opportunity to have a mind that is not full of future worries, past fears, or an ongoing list of to-dos. You deserve to be mindful rather than mind-full.

**Mindfulness.** When my son was four, he told me that mindfulness was "just doing what you are doing!" I always smile when I remember my sweet little boy sharing that definition, because really, it is so spot on. Mindfulness is really just that—paying attention to the present moment without judgment.

For my four-year-old, being mindful came naturally. He was fully absorbed in each action of the day, such as observing and discovering.

Another definition of mindfulness (beyond that of my then four-year-old) comes from Jon Kabat-Zinn.[38] He describes mindfulness as "the awareness that arises from paying attention, on purpose, in the present moment and non-judgmentally."

As adults, we seem to lose much of that mindful lens. However, we can regain and develop our mindful awareness through practices and tools that I will share in this chapter. The first practice that helped me cultivate a more mindful approach to life was beginning to meditate daily.

**Meditation.** Meditation is an opportunity to bring awareness to what is within (thoughts, breath, body) and without, in the space around you.

Meditation can be done sitting on a cushion or a chair. Meditation can also be practiced while lying down or walking.

Before we dive into the benefits of meditation, though, it is important to debunk some of the meditation myths and look at the science so that you can decide how/if meditation is a tool you would like to pursue.

# TOOL #1: UNDERSTAND THE MYTHS OF MEDITATION

In theory, meditation sounds simple. Many people think of meditation as sitting down and emptying the mind. The catch, though, is that this simplistic assumption about meditation is the same thing that prevents people from meditating in the first place.

You might think you should be able to sit with a clear mind, but when you try, you find the mind isn't still (so annoying, I know!).

Thus, you conclude that meditation is not for you. You think you can't meditate "well" like others can and quickly give up trying. Or maybe you haven't personally experienced the benefits of meditation, so you don't devote the time to making it a daily habit.

The first time I tried to meditate over fifteen years ago, I had grand plans of setting my timer for ten minutes. I quickly found my thoughts were so loud that I couldn't stand sitting another minute more. Not only did I not enjoy meditation, I never wanted to try again. Fortunately, I had a wise friend who encouraged me to start slowly and begin by setting a timer for three minutes and observing my thoughts instead of judging them.

As I mentioned in Section 1 of this book, people think six thousand to sixty thousand thoughts each day, and most of those thoughts are repetitive in nature. They are usually centered on what will happen in the future or on mistakes of the past.

The human mind is busy, and it is through meditation that you can begin to observe your thoughts the same way that a mountain sits still and observes the weather. Some days it is sunny and other days there is wind or rain; regardless, the mountain watches as the weather changes with each season. I had to be patient with my mind during meditation and expect that learning to meditate takes time. I had to learn to accept that some days would not be sunny (this is a lifelong learning that I continue to practice each day that I sit in meditation).

In fact, the more you learn about meditation, the more you realize that it is a practice that no one ever graduates from. It offers a daily calm, which you get each day that you meditate (kind of like taking vitamins—you can't just take your vitamin D once and expect it to have a lasting effect).

In the West, the origins, facts, and science behind meditation remain unknown to many. So, let's start with the basics by looking at the origins of meditation.

Meditation goes a long way back, but it is still a newer concept in the United States. In the twentieth century, meditation became more popular when a yogi, Swami Vivekananda, delivered a presentation to the Parliament of the World's Religions. Many years later, in the 1960s, there was a wave of studying the scientific benefits of meditation.

Despite the growing awareness of what meditation is and the positive benefits, many people still associate meditation as a religious or cultural practice (another myth). This perception of meditation being only for people of certain faiths, cultures, or spiritual practices is in fact false.

Truthfully, not only is meditation available to all people—even the most evolved meditators still have busy minds when they meditate! In Buddhism, these busy thoughts that one experiences while meditating are called the "monkey mind," referring to how thoughts jump around like monkeys swinging from branch to branch.

The difference between the novice meditator and the person who practices frequently is the person who practices brings more awareness to the mind. They can observe the monkey mind (just like the mountain), and with practice, befriend oneself and the mind rather than running away. The more you befriend your thoughts, the more you find calmness with them and in everyday life, resting in the reality of what is happening that very moment.

Another common meditation myth is that people should have a feeling of bliss when they meditate. Although there are times when I have personally felt very blissful during my meditation, it is also true that in the quiet I become aware of pain in my body, worries that I have been trying to avoid, and upsetting feelings. The purpose of meditation is not to be in a place of pure joy the entire time, but rather learn to give yourself care and attention.

When thoughts are loud, the body aches, and noises of the busy street outside your home drive you nutty, meditation can be very healing and an opportunity to practice self-compassion. Self-compassion is being kind to yourself when you suffer, feel as though you have failed, or have physical discomfort.

It is during meditation that you truly get to check in with your experience each day, offer yourself the support you need, and cultivate a practice of awareness. When you do this, it makes the stress from the rest of the day easier to navigate because you have taken care of your emotional needs.

If you are just beginning a practice, I invite you to throw away any expectations of what meditation needs to look like or how it should feel. A great way to begin meditation is to find a comfortable space to sit and focus on the inhale and exhale of your breath.

You can try to count 1-2-3 as you inhale and exhale slowly with a count of 1-2-3. Simply sit for a minute or two and observe your breath. This can be the first step in cultivating a meditation practice.

After examining these common meditation myths and how they deter people from trying to meditate, you may be inspired to go beyond the myths and find out if meditation is right for you (or maybe you have meditated in the past or meditate daily now and you want to increase your knowledge around meditation and time spent meditating each day; if so, awesome!).

The best way to dive into or boost your meditation practice is to set some healthy routines around it.

# TOOL #2: CULTIVATING YOUR MEDITATION PRACTICE

The first step is to get clear on *why* you want to meditate. Below, make a list of five to ten reasons you would like to commit your time to meditation.

*Why I Want to Meditate*

_____

_____

_____

_____

_____

_____

_____

_____

It is helpful to keep a list of the benefits close at hand. My list includes fewer obsessive thoughts, less stress and anxiety, better focus, and increased empathy and compassion for myself and others. Having a clear list of why meditation helps will encourage you to carve out the time to meditate daily (which is the second step).

Step two is to start your practice with a goal you know you can achieve. One minute a day for a month is a great way to start! Once you feel comfortable with that, you can go up to three minutes, then five, and so on. There is no rush, and it is best to move at a pace that feels achievable.

If you are already meditating but it is less consistent, decide how much time you can realistically give to meditation each day for thirty days. It is the daily habit that will make it stick, so set your goals as ones that you can achieve.

Over the past decade and a half, meditation is what has helped me create more of an internal calm. After I was really rooted in my meditation practice, I began to look at better ways to incorporate mindfulness into my life.

Now that we have examined some of the facts of meditation and reviewed a few of the benefits, I invite you to practice the guided meditation below.

While you do this, don't forget your facts of meditation!

» **A.** Meditation does not require an empty mind.

» **B.** It is available to everyone.

» **C.** Science also tells us there are many benefits of meditation.

» **Benefits of Meditation:** reduced stress, better emotional well-being, increased ability for self-regulation, less anxiety, increased self-awareness, better focus, may improve sleep, may help control pain, and can help cultivate a greater sense of kindness/gratitude

# TOOL #3: GUIDED MEDITATION

There are many forms and practices of meditation. If you are interested in exploring meditation further, I encourage you to sign up for my weekly Calming Newsletter at www.lauralinnknight.com, where I often share mindfulness and meditation tips. I also have personally found guided meditation apps to be a wonderful resource. One of my favorites is Insight Timer.

For this guided meditation, I will show you how to do a mindfulness meditation. Mindfulness meditation primarily works with breath as an anchor for the wandering mind. As you place your attention on your inhale and exhale, you will notice the mind drifting away from the breath and into other thoughts. This is normal and to be expected. When you notice that your mind has strayed, gently shift your attention back to your breath.

Let's begin.

**1.** Take a seat in a space that feels peaceful and safe for you. You may want to sit in a chair, sit on the ground with your legs in a crisscross position, or lie flat on your back.

**2.** Set a timer for a short period of time so that you can feel successful in today's practice. I began with three minutes. You may feel that you can do one minute, five minutes, or ten minutes. You decide what is right for you.

**3.** Close your eyes or find a place to focus a soft gaze of your eyes.

**4.** Become aware of your body. Notice what areas of your body feel tight, tense, or tired.

You can begin to bring this awareness of your body to the tips of your toes to begin. Simply notice how they feel and allow your breath to travel through your nose, down your throat, past your belly, down your legs, and into your toes.

For each part of the body that you bring your focus to in this meditation, I invite you to let your breath travel to that place.

How much time you are allowing for your meditation today will dictate how much time you want to spend on each area of your body (this practice is known as a body scan).

Let your awareness go from the tip of your toes into your feet, up your legs, into your groin, around your belly, through your right fingers, hands, and arm, into your chest, and down your left arm, hands, and fingers.

Bring your awareness now into your neck, to the base of your skull, and up into your head.

Allow your breath to act as a permission slip, giving each part of your body the license to relax, let go, and melt into a restful state.

**5.** Return to your breath, watching the deep inhale and slow exhale.

**6.** Offer kindness to the mind if it wanders, offer kindness to yourself as the caretaker for the beautiful humans you are raising and the joy and pain that comes with that, and offer kindness to yourself for trying your best in this moment.

**7.** When you are ready, open your eyes or lift your gaze. Become aware of the space you are in and notice how you feel after having just completed your meditation practice for the day.

**8.** Place your hand on your heart or one hand on your heart and one hand on your belly. Offer yourself a compassionate statement that you can take with you for the day. For example, "I am proud of myself," "I am trying my best today," or "With each breath, I inhale more love and patience and exhale perfectionism and pain."

**9.** Congratulations! Whether this was your first meditation or you are a regular to the practice, you carved out time just for yourself—a time that shows you are committed to growing and learning! Woo-hoo!

Meditation is a wonderful tool for a few minutes of each day. And, as discussed, it has numerous benefits that will support you and your family.

But what about the other hours of the day, when you are not sitting in meditation? Let's learn tools of mindfulness for those times when you are interacting with your children, family, coworkers, and the larger outside world.

# TOOL #4: MINDFULNESS FOR DAILY LIVING

In 2019, I was invited to present globally during Expedia's Wellness Month on the topic of mindful parenting. The takeaway from my presentation was that when we parents have a daily mindfulness practice, we are more likely to show up in a loving and present way for our children.

As I explore what mindfulness in daily life looks like, I will share similar tools to those I presented in May 2019, plus many more practices that I have learned, taught, and experienced along the way.

Mindfulness has many definitions. Here are a few that I have created through my own teachings and that other experts in the field have developed. Because mindfulness sounds simplistic but takes some work to cultivate, I have found having multiple working definitions helpful as a reminder for this daily practice.

## MINDFULNESS DEFINITIONS

*Mindfulness is being in the present moment—here and now—one breath at a time.*

*Mindfulness is bringing equality to our thoughts and current experience.*

*Mindfulness is awareness of the present moment without judgment.*

All these definitions have the same fundamental teaching at their root: nonjudgmental awareness of what is happening in the present moment. I invite you to write one of the definitions above on a sticky note and place it somewhere in your home for a daily inspirational reminder to practice mindfulness.

Now, you might be thinking, why would I do that? Why would I want to take the time to practice mindfulness each day? This is a great question, one that deserves an answer. Let me start by sharing a personal story and then some scientific facts about mindfulness.

In my home, my husband and I tend to agree on most of our parenting practices and rules. He very sweetly attended one of the first parenting workshops I ever taught, and he also listens to me talk about the copious amount of parenting books I read each month.

One area, however, that we do not always see eye to eye on is screen time for our children. One interesting fact about me is that I am not a television or movie watcher. I have very little interest in watching shows, and I tend to be very cautious about what I want to let my children watch. My husband, on the other hand, loves watching movies and really enjoys watching shows with the kids. To boot, the shows he likes to watch tend to be different from what I would like. To be honest, I would probably just have my kids watch *Curious George* for the rest of their lives (#truestory), so it is probably good that my husband balances me out a little in this way.

Now that you know the backstory around my parenting views on this subject (and your knowledge from Chapter 5 on screen time), you can imagine the feelings that may have come out fast and strong when my husband suggested he watch *Mission Impossible* with our then eight-year-old son.

Don't get me wrong, even though I don't tend to watch many movies, I will always hold a special place in my heart for this action-packed series. But should my young child be watching them? *No!*

My son and husband were watching the trailer to decide if they would rent the movie. I noticed the fear of their watching a movie outside of our family agreement rise in my body. My mama-bear was growing stronger within me by the second. I could feel my heart starting to beat faster, my body becoming warmer, and cortisol beginning to release within me. I have had this experience before when my children were younger and my mindfulness practice was less tuned. The result? Me yelling, shaming, blaming, and sometimes having a full-on fit.

On this particular day, though, I was in a different space. Since I have devoted many years now to daily meditation and mindfulness practice (plus I work hard on our first parenting tool of self-regulation), I approached it from a calmer place. Before I said anything to my husband, I observed the feelings that felt really strong in my body. I was curious about where I felt each feeling in my body. I didn't judge myself for my big feelings that were rising, but rather allowed some deep breaths to offer comfort to the fear and frustration.

It didn't take long to have that internal check-in, and then use calm words to share my view on the appropriateness of the movie. When I am not in reaction, my husband is better able to hear me (I would say that is true for all humans, right?). We respond better when the lower part of our brain isn't threatened by an angry tone or harsh words. We picked a different movie that we all agreed on and had a lovely Saturday.

My takeaway from that experience? Mindfulness makes self-regulation easier and more accessible in daily life. And having a mindfulness practice allows parents to have the internal harmony and balance we so very much crave (thus creating an external home environment that is calmer).

Additionally, Jon Kabat-Zinn says that "Mindfulness is a way of befriending ourselves and our experience." You can see how this was also true in the story I shared above. When I observed my big feelings without judgment or reaction, I was befriending myself and my experience because I was able to accept my feelings in a kind way. I was then able to communicate with confidence and compassion rather than fear (a historical fear that arises in me when I don't feel heard).

You can see how layered our feelings can be. How our daily responses to our family are often driven by past events in our own lives, our own feelings of worthiness, past wounds and traumas, and our personal beliefs. Mindfulness gives a lens to view our internal world so that we don't create undue suffering in our outer world.

This is one simple story of many that I have personally experienced with my mindfulness practice. You can see many of the benefits of mindfulness interwoven, but I want to go beyond my own personal experience now and share the benefits that experts in the field of mindfulness have found to be true.

## BENEFITS OF MINDFULNESS

» Mindfulness reduces anxiety and may also improve stress reactivity.[39]

» Mindfulness holds promise for treating depression (especially using mindfulness-based cognitive therapy).[40]

» Mindfulness can decrease the suffering many women feel around body dissatisfaction and help increase body satisfaction.[41]

» Mindfulness meditation enhances the ability to sustain attention.[42]

» Mindfulness meditation improves emotion regulation and reduces drug abuse.[43]

With so many benefits to mindfulness, you may wonder why everyone hasn't begun a daily mindfulness practice. In truth, many people don't know where or how to start their practice. Additionally, those of you who have already learned mindfulness tools may find yourself forgetting to use them often. Sharon Salzberg, a well-known mindfulness teacher, says, "Mindfulness isn't difficult, we just need to remember to do it."

I will bring this chapter to an end by sharing practical mindfulness tools that you can incorporate into your daily life. And I will encourage you to write yourself a sticky note, set a reminder in your phone, or buddy up with a friend to remind yourself to make these tools part of the new habits you are creating so that you can have a calmer and less reactive family life.

# TOOL #5: SIX MINDFULNESS PRACTICES

## MINDFUL EATING

Growing up, I don't remember if I was a particularly fast eater. I honestly never noticed, and no one ever mentioned it to me. After having my children, however, I became a speed eater. I probably should have competed in an eating contest or two, because my ability to scarf food down was unbelievable. Not only did I notice the quickness of my eating, but others were also astonished by how fast I would finish a meal. With so much to do in a day, I couldn't make time for slowly chewing my food (let alone sitting down for breakfast and lunch).

When my children were ages two and four, I noticed some increased anxiety in my life. It was during this time that a friend of mine suggested I practice mindful eating as a way to incorporate a pause into my day to help reduce stress.

I knew that trying mindful eating for a whole meal would be too much to begin with. So, I decided to start with a snack. I was apprehensive at first, but I discovered that practicing mindful eating for one snack each day began to give me a nice pause. And the more that I paused, the more I wanted to incorporate more pauses in my life. I quickly went from mindful eating of just a snack to mindful eating of many more meals each day.

If you are curious about mindful eating and want to start your own daily practice, mindful eating is paying attention to each bite of food without judgment.

When you eat mindfully, you may ask yourself: What does the food smell like? What does the food taste like? What is the texture of the food? What tastes do you notice on your tongue before the food goes down your throat?

If you have a raisin in your house (or an almond), I invite you to put this book down and go get it. Once it is in your hands, come back to this chapter and read the following directions:

» Rub the piece of food between your fingers. What does it feel like?

» Close your eyes and smell the food. Do you notice any distinct smells?

» Place the food in your mouth, but do not chew it. Instead, let it roll around on your tongue. What does it feel like in your mouth? Can you taste anything yet?

» When you take your first bite, notice how your teeth feel biting into the food. Now is there more of a taste?

» Notice the process of thoroughly chewing your food. What does it feel like as it passes through your mouth and down your throat?

You have just practiced eating mindfully. This is a really fun activity to do with your child as well, and there is a fun children's version included in Section 2 of this chapter.

## MINDFUL CLEANING

"If while washing dishes, we think only of the cup of tea that awaits us, thus hurrying to get the dishes out of the way as if they were a nuisance, then we are not 'washing the dishes to wash the dishes.'

What's more, we **are not alive** during the time we are washing the dishes."—Thich Nhat Hanh

Most of us are not present in our daily chores. In fact, my mother-in-law and I were just joking that my phone was so dirty because I was watching both kids, making dinner, cleaning up, and holding my phone to my ear while my makeup smudged off on it. Although this was an exaggeration, on some days, it isn't far from the truth.

Folding laundry, washing dishes, sweeping. . .none of these have ever been high on my top ten favorite activities. And, although mindful cleaning may not make these everyday tasks become our favorite things to do, can we use the simplicity of everyday chores as a teacher in being present? Can we truly focus on what we are doing *now*, rather than multitasking or daydreaming of what is to happen next/what happened in the past?

Thich Nhat Hanh's quote reminds us to be present with the activity at hand. To be alive in the moment of the activity!

The next time you are, for example, washing the dishes, I invite you to notice how the water feels on your hands, what the soap looks like and smells like in the sink, and the motions your hands make as your rinse and dry each dish. Can you bring awareness to your breath as you engage fully in the dishwashing process?

Try this for the next month as you do various chores around your home. Notice how your perspective changes as you adopt this new lens for your daily to-dos.

## MINDFUL SELF-COMPASSION

When I first learned about mindfulness, I thought that to observe the body and mind with equanimity meant to push my thoughts and feelings away. Over time, I found myself frustrated with mindfulness because avoiding feelings is not only unhealthy, but also unsustainable.

Then, when I was getting my certification to become a mindfulness and meditation teacher, I purchased the *Mindful Self-Compassion Workbook* by Christopher Germer and Kristin Neff. The book radically changed my relationship with mindfulness and with myself.

Mindful self-compassion taught me to observe my thoughts and feelings, and with that observation, to *embrace* the feelings that I felt. It taught me to offer myself kind words and/or gestures (e.g., a hand on my heart) when big feelings would come to visit.

Kristin Neff says, "As soon as you notice you're suffering, you automatically embrace yourself with compassion."

Although I have written about self-compassion throughout the book, I wanted to add it again here as a reminder that this is a very powerful tool that will help heal your relationship to yourself, your old wounds, and your traumas. In turn, this self-compassion will translate to how you interact with your children and in all relationships in your life.

If you would like to start a daily self-compassion practice, I encourage you to check out the *Mindful Self-Compassion Workbook*. I also encourage you to begin placing a hand on your heart in your meditation, to embrace and honor your feelings when they arise, and to practice an internal dialogue with yourself that allows for compassionate talk.

Mindful self-compassion is not about pushing "bad" feelings away or trying to talk yourself into feeling better when you are upset. Instead, you are treating yourself like you would a friend (empathetically, without trying to change what is).

## MINDFUL MEDITATION

We have covered meditation and mindful meditation throughout this chapter, but I am still including it here in your list of tools as a reminder of what a powerful tool you have at your disposal each and every day.

Remember, mindful meditation is bringing awareness to what you are sensing and feeling in the moment. You can do this when you intentionally sit down to meditate, but you can also take breaks throughout the day to pause and practice. This is an especially helpful tool when you are feeling overwhelmed with your child.

Have compassion for yourself as you observe your internal experience. Place a hand on your heart and trust that you are safe to observe and feel whatever arises.

# MINDFUL LISTENING

Mindful listening can have two components. The first is to listen to another person without criticism, judgment, or distraction. I have noticed over the years how much pulls at me when I am trying to listen to my children and my partner. There seems to always be a phone buzzing, a task pulling my attention away, or my own monkey mind wanting me to leap from topic to topic. Practicing mindful listening with those around me can strengthen my relationships and help me create longer-lasting bonds.

The other type of mindful listening is when you are not in conversation with someone, but rather listening to sounds in the environment around you. I find this tool to be particularly helpful with the adults and children that I work with who have anxiety. Teaching a person to tune into the cars driving by, the birds chirping, or the sound of distant music playing gives their mind an opportunity to focus on the present moment in an objective way. This can help to steady the mind and calm the body.

# MINDFUL WALKING

The last mindfulness tool that I would like to share in this chapter is mindful walking. Mindful walking may be one of my favorite mindfulness tools (although I have already said that about other mindfulness tools throughout the book and in this chapter!). In all fairness, it is hard to say which tools are my favorite because all these tools hold a special place in my heart. I came to mindfulness out of a need—a need to reduce my stress, be more present with my family, react less to my children, create more connected relationships, and have a deeper and kinder relationship with myself. All of the tools I share with you are in this book because they helped me achieve those goals (and more). Mindful walking has been a saving grace for me in difficult times because it allows me to really get grounded and be present with nature and the space around me.

Mindful walking can be done in as little as five minutes a day or longer. It is a practice of using all your senses while you take each step.

When I was at Spirit Rock Meditation Center in Woodacre, California, I did a mindful-walking exercise where students walked either outside or inside, counting each step until they reached ten steps. Once we had taken ten steps, we would turn around and walk the other way. This back and forth of counting our steps and syncing that with the breath was incredibly relaxing. And, the cool thing is, you can do this anywhere (you don't have to be at a meditation center to reap the benefits)!

Counting your steps is one approach to mindful walking. Another approach is to go for a walk or a hike, and rather than counting steps, keep directing the mind back to what you see, feel, hear, and smell as you walk. Of course, the mind will wander during your walk, so be gentle with yourself as you notice the wandering mind, and redirect it back to present awareness.

Continue to use these six mindfulness tools in combination with establishing a meditation routine. Try it each day for at least one month and notice how you feel at the end of month.

For now, write the date below and rate your current mood on a scale of 1–10. Bookmark this page and come back to it after a month of going from mind-full to mindful. Write the new date and your current mood.

| Date | Current Mood Scale (1–10) |
|---|---|
|  |  |
|  |  |

# FOR YOUR KIDS

Mindfulness is being taught in schools across the country, and that brings a mindfulness and meditation teacher like myself great joy.

With that said, though, sometimes mindfulness can become parent/teacher directed instead of child desired. Because children are actually quite mindful by nature, the tools here play on the mindful tendencies they already have and make mindfulness a "want to" rather than a "have to."

The rest of this chapter will be written for you to read to your child.

**Dear Friends,**

Wow, you are almost to the end of the book, and by now, you have so many really amazing tools that you have learned. I am super proud of you, and I hope that you are proud of yourself too.

This chapter is about mindfulness and meditation. You may have heard of both. If you have, you may like them, think they are annoying, or feel neutral to the ideas.

Your parents are learning a lot about mindfulness and meditation, so if you want to ask them questions about it or want to share with them what you already know, now would be a really good time to tell them what you know. You can also ask them questions.

When you are done talking, come back to this part of the book so I can share some fun ways to practice mindfulness and meditation.

# MINDFULNESS

When my son was four, he told me that "mindfulness is doing what you are doing!" That is a really good definition for a four-year-old, and pretty spot on. Mindfulness is being aware of what you are doing (which most kids are really good at). As you get older, though, you may start to notice that video games are pulling your attention, your mind may worry about what a friend said, or you may get nervous about a test at school. All of this is really normal, and mindfulness is a way to teach your mind to stay in the moment rather than running off with your thoughts.

There are some ways you can teach your mind to do this, and the result will be that you are calmer, more focused, and may even feel happier. Below I share some mindfulness tools that I think you will really like!

# TOOL #1: MINDFUL BODY SCAN

I love fairy tales and nursery rhymes. When my kids were little, I wanted to teach them to do a mindful body scan (which means noticing how your body feels). I thought it would be fun to pretend that Humpty Dumpty from the nursery rhyme had done a body scan after the king's horses and the king's men put him back together again.

This is how I taught my kids to do a body scan, and this is a fun way that you can do one too!

## HUMPTY DUMPTY

Once upon a time, more than one hundred years ago, a gigantic egg named Humpty Dumpty climbed onto a brick wall and accidentally fell down. A story was written about him that children around the world read to this day.

Would you like to hear it?

Humpty Dumpty sat on a wall,

Humpty Dumpty had a great fall.

All the king's horses and all the king's men couldn't put
Humpty together again.

I like to be positive, so let's pretend that Humpty Dumpty was one lucky egg, and the children of the royal court came to his rescue. They glued his shell together again.

Humpty Dumpty had to sit so still, even though the cracks were ouchies! He felt scared and sad. And it was really hard not to wiggle.

Fortunately, the king's horses and the king's men invited Humpty to lie down on the king's magic carpet while the glue dried. They said, "Close your eyes, Humpty Dumpty, and take a deep breath through your nose, all the way down to your belly. Puff out your belly, big as a ball. Release the breath out through your nose."

"But my cracks ache," Humpty said.

"Name the part that hurts the most," they said. "Take another deep breath through your nose into your belly and imagine your warm breath moving to the ouchie. Can you feel your muscles relax? Now release the breath out through your nose."

A few minutes later, Humpty was good to go. Humpty Dumpty smiled because he felt all better after his fall! It is your turn now to learn how to feel better whenever you get an ouchie or feel sad or scared.

## BODY SCAN FOR YOU

Find a comfortable place to lie down on your back.

Let your arms fall to your sides.

Close your eyes, or keep them open, and gaze at a spot on the ceiling.

Follow along as your grown-up guides you through a body scan.

Take a deep breath in through your nose and let all the air out through your mouth.

Take three more big belly breaths, allowing each breath to fill up your belly with air.

Think about how the air feels moving in and out of your body. Is it warm? Is it cool? Does it tickle your nose?

Notice your belly rising up and down, up and down.

Place a hand on your belly and notice your hand rising up and down,

up and down,

as you breathe in and out,

in and out.

Now let's focus friendly attention to other parts of your body.

Start with your toes. Notice: Do they feel warm or cold? Are they wiggly or still? Notice how your toes and feet feel right now, at this moment.

Now, let's move from your toes to your knees to your shoulders to your head.

If you have an ouchie anywhere on your body, pay friendly attention to how it feels.

Notice your ankles.

Notice your knees.

Notice your thighs.

Notice your hips.

Notice your butt.

Notice your belly.

Notice your chest.

Notice your shoulders.

Notice your arms.

Notice your wrists.

Notice your hands.

Notice your fingers.

Bring your breath back up your arms.

Notice your neck.

Notice your face.

Notice the top of your head.

For the next minute, let go and be still.

Notice the clothes on your body.

Notice how the ground or bed feels underneath you.

Good job, Friend. You can do this body scan anytime—indoors or outside—to help you feel better when you are hurt or when you feel sad, mad, angry, or scared.

　　　　**BREAK FREE FROM REACTIVE PARENTING**

Just like Humpty Dumpty, you can always notice, relax, and feel better together again!

# TOOL #2: MINDFUL BREATH

We have practiced using your breath throughout this book as a tool for calming your body and mind. The breath is such a fantastic tool because you have your breath with you everywhere you go.

You have learned to take in a big Huff and let out a slow Puff with Wolf! You have practiced counting your breaths: one, two, three!

You have even done fun breathing games where you blow soap bubbles in your hands or pretend your fingers are birthday cake candles that you are blowing out.

Now, I would like to invite you to write down three more ways you could use your breath. In the space below, write and draw how you could use your breath.

# TOOL #3: MINDFUL-ALIEN EATING

Did you know that you can practice eating mindfully? I didn't know about mindful eating until I was all grown up, but now that I have done it for a while, I think it is really fun. Plus, I find it makes my food taste even better.

Let's practice mindful eating with a raisin. If you really don't like raisins, you could use a nut or a strawberry, but for my directions below I will say "raisin" to make it simple.

I want you to imagine that you are an alien who has never been to Earth or tasted the food we have here. You have just landed on our planet in your spaceship and walked into a grocery store, where you bought a box of raisins. You opened the box and are now holding the raisin in your hand.

I want you to examine this raisin in your hand like it is something you have never ever seen before. Really look at it closely. Is it smooth or rough? Is it bumpy? What color is it? What does it feel like?

Put the raisin up to your nose. Does it have a smell to it?

Now, slowly put the raisin in your mouth. Don't chew it yet or swallow it! Let the raisin roll around on your tongue. What does that feel like?

When you are ready, take a slow bite into the raisin. What does it taste like? Is it sweet? Do you like the taste on your tongue?

Keep chewing your raisin and then notice it as it goes down your throat.

What do you think about this food that humans have on Earth? Would you like to try another one?

Let's stop being aliens now. As a human, what did you notice when you ate the raisin? I am always surprised by how sweet the raisin seems to taste when I taste it slowly and bring all my attention to it. The first time I did this, even though I had eaten lots and lots of raisins in my life, I felt like this was the first time I had really experienced the way it felt and tasted.

You can do this with all your food. You can also suggest that your family has mindful family dinners where you all really notice the taste, smell, and texture of your food!

# TOOL #4: MINDFUL WALKING

I bet you walk all the time! You walk at school, you walk around the house, and you may even go on walks with your grown-ups! Now, of course, some kids don't walk because they are in a wheelchair, or they need special help getting around. If you are a kid who gets from place to place in a unique way, then this activity is still for you!

The next time you are going from one place to the next, I want you to notice the sounds that you hear. What is the temperature like around you? Is it hot? Cold? What do you see or smell?

If your feet are touching the ground, what does it feel like with each step? If you are in a wheelchair, what does it feel like as you glide across the floor or go on the ground outside? Can you count your breaths, steps, or seconds as you go? This can be a great tool for when you are having big feelings like anger, sadness, or fear. The more you notice the space around you, the calmer your body becomes.

# TOOL #5: MEDITATION

Meditation can look different for everyone, but I like to think of it as noticing your body, breath, and thoughts.

In meditation, you can sit or lie down on the ground as you pay attention to how you are feeling and what you are thinking.

When I first started to meditate, I noticed that I had a lot of thoughts. Now, that isn't a bad thing, but sometimes I didn't want to have so many thoughts racing through my mind. I learned to quiet my mind by focusing on my breath. Yes, the breath! By now, you are probably seeing just how powerful the breath can be (it is like a superpower that so many people don't even know they have). For the meditation we are going to do today, we will count five breaths and then start back at the number one once we reach the fifth breath.

If your mind starts to wander, you can gently remind it to keep counting your breaths. Be kind to your mind the same way you would help a kitten that was wandering away in the backyard. You would pick that kitty up and bring it back into the house and close the door. We can treat our mind just as nicely.

When you are ready, find a place to sit comfortably or lie on the ground on your back.

Close your eyes or find a place to stare at softly.

Take a deep breath in through your nose and let the air go down into your belly. If you want, you can place your hand on your belly.

Now, let that breath out through your mouth nice and slowly. That is breath number one.

Again, take a deep breath in through your nose and let the air go down into your belly.

Let that breath out through your mouth nice and slowly. That is breath number two.

Again, take a deep breath in through your nose and let the air go down into your belly.

Let that breath out through your mouth nice and slowly. That is breath number three.

Again, take a deep breath in through your nose and let the air go down into your belly.

Let that breath out through your mouth nice and slowly. That is breath number four.

Again, take a deep breath in through your nose and let the air go down into your belly.

Let that breath out through your mouth nice and slowly. That is breath number five.

If your mind was thinking about something else, that is okay. Just let the thought go and come back to the breath you were counting (or start again at number one if you lost your place).

You can count your breaths for as long as you want to.

As you are counting your breaths, you may notice how your body is feeling. You may notice how your body feels after your meditation.

What about your thoughts? Is your mind as busy thinking as it was before your meditation, or have your thoughts slowed down a little?

I like to end my meditation with an appreciation about myself and my life. I might say something like, "I am so grateful for being a kind friend and I am grateful that I have a loving family."

What is something that you appreciate about yourself and your life?

Friends, I know I have said this many times throughout the book, but I just have to tell you again how proud I am of you for learning all of these tools! You are learning things that many grown-ups don't know how to do, and these teachings will help you now and throughout your entire life.

Thank you for doing that meditation with me, and thank you for reading this book with your grown-up!

# CHAPTER 10

# HOW TO START AND END YOUR DAY

Have you ever noticed how classrooms have consistent daytime routines? This is because teachers know that routines create safety, familiarity, order, and trust for children.

Of course, it would not be possible for our homes to have the same amount of time set aside for daily routines that a classroom has. That wouldn't work with the flexibility we need in our homes, and the rigidity wouldn't be helpful for our children. However, having a morning and night routine can benefit us and our children greatly.

For parents, starting your day with a self-care practice, a journal prompt, or a mini-meditation will set the tone for how you want to show up with your family for the day. Ending your day with a gratitude list, some time without screens, and a little self-reflection will keep the bedtime worries away and boost your mood.

In Chapter 7, we explored the logistical tactics around morning and bedtime routines for children. This chapter will go beyond the logistics to act as a guide so you can create a routine that will help your well-being (and your child's well-being too).

It is now time for you to take everything you have learned in this book and put it all together in a way that is meaningful and helpful for *you*!

Reading an entire book these days can feel like a lot, and honestly, most parents I know can't seem to find the time to read anymore. The fact that you have made it this far should be celebrated. It shows your commitment to your family, your child, and yourself, and marks a turning point in your parenting journey where you can stop reacting and start thriving.

CONGRATULATIONS!

You now have a toolbox that will help you in the stickiest parenting situations. You are like a ninja—you have learned one tool, action, and behavior at a time. You have gone on a mission to discover more about yourself and your child. And now, you will find all your tools will begin to flow from you seamlessly. You will thrive under the most difficult of circumstances (well, at least most of the time)! You will be a Ninja Mom or a Ninja Dad or a Ninja Caregiver, not letting the difficulties of parenthood weigh you down like they once did because you are wise, dedicated, and full of master parenting moves.

However, this newfound state will only last if you choose to maintain it each day. You cannot give to your child if you aren't giving to yourself first. You cannot stay less reactive if you are drained, exhausted, and uncentered.

That is why Chapter 9 introduced mindfulness and meditation to you. We must find our habits that fill us up and center us. And don't despair, if mindfulness or meditation isn't your jam, that is okay! Try walking each day, pick up a paintbrush and create something, knit a sweater—do *you* and set aside that time to do it.

In Chapter 10, we put it all together. You have your list of tools from Chapter 8 (make a copy or two and have them around for when you are feeling overwhelmed). You have your self-regulation dos and don'ts checklist from Chapter 2. And now you are ready to add the remaining tools for how best to start and end your days.

# TOOL #1: CARVE OUT TIME EACH MORNING FOR MEDITATION

For this tool, I am going to use the term "meditation," but I would like to reiterate that if meditation isn't what you feel drawn to right now, then you can substitute anything that feels grounding for you.

Substitute meditation ideas include:

» Listening to a positive talk online, as an audiobook, or via any other platform that allows you to access inspiring talks

» Drawing, painting, or creating

» Mindful breathing

» Mindful walking

» Sitting for five minutes with soft music playing in the background

» Practicing yoga poses

» Lying down with a pillow on your belly and watching it rise and fall with your breath

The idea here is that before you run out of your room and start fixing breakfast, packing lunches, and trying to get your kids out the door, you build in a pause to honor yourself, get your body into a peaceful state, and set a tone for how you want the rest of your day to go.

Although this sounds simple in theory, I know just how hard it is to carve out five minutes of this type of practice when most of us have such busy mornings.

When my children were young, I would often meditate with one of them curled up in my lap or both of them sitting right there next to me. I knew it wasn't the quiet meditation I had envisioned, but it worked (and, as a bonus, my kids are really open to meditation because it was modeled for them from a very young age).

As always, be easy on yourself, but do set a timer for a few minutes each morning to engage in this habit. Set your alarm for ten minutes earlier than you normally wake up if you need to just so you are sure to get the time in.

# TOOL #2: MORNING QUIET REFLECTION WITH JOURNAL PROMPT

This can come right at the end of your morning meditation, or you can circle back to it after breakfast. Whenever you do it, just try not to let the morning slip away from you without taking a moment for this tool.

In keeping with the understanding that we are all busy, busy, busy, don't worry—this doesn't need to be a long activity.

I suggest setting a timer for anywhere from three to ten minutes when you can sit quietly and write down the answers to the following journal prompts:

**1.** *What do you appreciate about yourself today?*

_____

_____

**2.** *What do you appreciate about your child/children?*

_____

_____

**3.** *What do you appreciate about anyone else who is helping you raise your child/children (this could be your spouse, a family member, a close friend, etc.)?*

_____

_____

Many years ago, when my children were little, I had built up some resentment. I was not feeling like the best version of myself with my body having been loaned out to make my beautiful babies and my work life transitioning from being a classroom teacher to a stay-at-home mother.

I answered the three questions above daily for several months and noticed how things began to shift significantly in my life.

I am a firm believer that as my internal world changes, my outside world reflects my state of being.

# TOOL #3: MORNING GRATITUDE RITUAL

This tool is different from tool #2 in that it is meant to be shared aloud with your family.

Each morning as you are driving your kids to school in the car, doing the dishes, or eating breakfast, take the time to say aloud something you are grateful for about each member of your family. This sets the tone of love and kindness in your home, and it also will serve to create wonderful habits of gratitude in your children.

# TOOL #4: EVENING THANK-YOU BOX

Find a shoe box or a leftover Amazon box, get out your colored markers and stickers, and start decorating! Your evening thank-you box is for you to extend your morning gratitude practice to the end of the day. You can write down on a piece of paper everything that you are grateful for and fill your box until it is stuffed. Then, after you have filled it completely, sit down and read through all your lists. You might be surprised by just how much is going well in your life!

This exercise can also be done for things that you are worried about. You can give thanks in advance for a situation you are fearful about being resolved. You can give thanks for the healing of a strained friendship or the healing of an illness. Follow your heart with this activity and make your thank-you box special for you.

# TOOL #5: HEALTHY EVENING HABITS

Just like we maintain our car, we need to maintain our bodies and minds. If we neglect to get our car's oil changed, wash it, or put gas in it—our car will be a big hot mess. If we stay up way too late, eat unhealthy food at night, spend our evenings scrolling through social media and feeling low afterward, then the mornings are going to be tough.

And, if our mornings are tough, then practicing the first three tools from this chapter is going to feel nearly impossible. We must think of this as a cycle. Each action from the morning affects the rest of our day, into our evening. Each action of the evening will dictate how we feel in the morning. The cycle continues until we decide to change it.

Because you are breaking free from reactive parenting, starting fresh in your life, and looking to show up differently, then you must examine what habits are benefiting or hindering you.

In the space below, write down evening habits that you would like to change and new habits that you would like to include after your children go to bed.

One habit that my husband and I have changed in our home over the years is to stop using devices after 10 p.m. We don't always adhere to this, and sometimes we need to make exceptions, but it is a healthy rule of thumb that works for us.

Another habit I have is writing down a few sentences each day in a journal about what our family did that day. I have done this for four years now, and I love looking back on all our special moments.

I also have the habit of looking at the moon in the evenings, as the moon is something that always reminds me to be grateful for my time on this planet. I used to see the moon from my meditation seat in my room when we lived in California. I don't have that where we are now, so I have to make the extra effort to go see the moon as much as I can. It is always worth the effort.

What habits would you like to have at night? Maybe they will be similar to mine, or maybe they will be completely different. Either way, it is okay. This is your opportunity to try new things and see what sticks.

*Healthy Evening Habits I Want to Incorporate*

_____

_____

_____

_____

_____

*Habits I Want to Change*

_____

_____

_____

_____

_____

I am excited to see how you feel as you begin to try these tools in your life.

I'm also so excited for this next new chapter of your life, and I believe wholeheartedly that you have the power within you to create the meaningful changes you want to see!

I will leave you with a few inspiring quotes that have helped me along the way, and that I hope will inspire you too.

> "I alone cannot change the world, but I can cast a
> stone across the waters to create many ripples."
>
> —Mother Theresa

> "Be the change that you wish to see in the world."
>
> —Mahatma Gandhi

"If you don't like something, change it. If you
can't change it, change your attitude."
—Maya Angelou

"The world as we have created it is a process of our thinking.
It cannot be changed without changing our thinking."
—Albert Einstein

"When patterns are broken, new worlds emerge."
—Tuli Kupferberg

"The greatest discovery of all time is that a person can
change his future by merely changing his attitude."
—Oprah Winfrey

# FOR YOUR KIDS

Your child is never too young to start creating healthy morning and bedtime routines that will last a lifetime. This chapter isn't simply about brushing teeth in the morning and taking a bath at night. Instead, we focus on the important check-ins we can create with our children at night and how setting intentions with our children before they leave the house can give them the confidence boost, support, and connection they need to thrive for that school day.

After reading this chapter, packed with morning ideas and nightly tips, kids will have a fun time figuring out what routines they want to try out!

The rest of this chapter will be written for you to read with your child.

**Dear Friends,**

Wow, you and your grown-up made it to the last chapter of this book. I am so proud of all your hard work, and I hope that you are proud of yourself too!

You have learned so many tools and know much more than I ever did when I was your age. I wish I had learned the tools you now have to calm your body down, take care of yourself when you are sad or scared, work through arguments with your sibling or friend, and so much more.

I hope you can take a moment to congratulate yourself for taking the time to learn all this new information (or practice things you might have been learning in school and at home). Again, I really am very proud of you.

For the last part of this chapter, I am going to share tools for how to start and end your day. The way that you start your day is important because it will help your mind get into a positive mindset for whatever comes along that day. How you end your day is equally as important, because this will help you go to bed with a happy heart and a more relaxed mind.

Here are six tools for how to start and end your day.

# TOOL #1: MORNING GRATITUDE AT BREAKFAST

As we have learned in this book, it is easy for our minds to slip into negative thoughts or miss out on all the good that is happening throughout each and every day. When we set aside time to pay special attention to the things we are grateful for, we begin to notice more and more things that make us happy, feel good, and give us appreciation for all the small things that are going well.

Make gratitude part of your morning routine by sharing one thing that you are grateful for at the breakfast table. The gratitude might be about something that has happened recently, happened a long time ago, or something you are excited about happening in the future. Each person at the table can take a turn sharing their gratitude for the day.

Hip, hip, hooray!

# TOOL #2: THREE SIMPLE MORNING STRETCHES

Focusing on a good stretch through yoga is a wonderful way to help give your mind space to help release big feelings you're experiencing or just get you in a positive mood to start your day.

Do these three kid-friendly yoga poses with your grown-up or on your own.

# DOWNWARD DOG

## DIRECTIONS

**1.** Begin on your hands and knees.

**2.** Walk your hands forward just a bit.

**3.** Tuck your toes, straighten your knees, and lift your hips up toward the ceiling or the sky.

**4.** Relax your heels toward the floor.

**5.** Let your head be soft between your arms.

# TREE POSE

## DIRECTIONS

**1.** Stand straight and tall.

**2.** Find a place for your eyes to focus on (this will help keep you from wobbling as much in the pose).

**3.** Take a slow breath out and bring your left foot up to the inside part of your right leg, above or below your knee.

**4.** Make your right leg as strong as you can, imagining it is the root of the tree going into the ground.

**5.** Slowly lift your arms out and above your head, or keep them together in front of your heart.

## CAT AND COW POSE

## DIRECTIONS

**1.** Begin on your hands and knees.

**2.** Spread your fingers. Check that your shoulders and elbows are lined up over your hands and your hips are over your knees.

**3.** Breathe out, drop your head, pull your tummy up, and tuck your spine. This is the Cat Pose.

**4.** Inhale to come back up to your first position with your flat back (this is called tabletop position).

**5.** For Cow Pose, look up to the ceiling or sky and let your belly sink down toward the ground.

**6.** Take a few deep breaths and then go back to your tabletop position.

To make these poses extra silly and fun, make noises when you do them!

What do you think a tree sounds like? Or can you moo like a cow or bark like a dog?

# TOOL #3: MINI MORNING STORY

Do you love telling or hearing stories? I know my kids particularly love hearing a really good story.

Sometimes we play a fun game in the car on the way to school, called two truths and one lie. The way that you play is each person takes a turn telling two things that are true about them and one thing that is not true. Everyone in the car has to guess what the lie is. It is a really fun way to hear stories about your family members or interesting things about them that you may not have known already.

Want to play a round with me? Here are my two truths and a lie. See if you can guess which one is the lie.

**1.** One time when I was thirteen, I went into the three great pyramids of Egypt with my mom. While I was there, I rode on the back of a camel.

**2.** I do *not* like Brussel sprouts at all.

**3.** When I was little, I went to a very special creek that we called hot and cold creek. It was called hot and cold creek because one side of the creek was cold like a normal river, but the other side of the river was hot because underneath the water were special hot springs that warmed up that side of the creek. I would swim with my mom from one side of the creek to the other to cool down when I was hot and warm up when I was cold.

What do you think was the lie?

The lie was #2, about Brussel sprouts. I actually *love* Brussel sprouts (and so do my kids).

Another way that we tell stories in the morning is by sharing special memories we have from when we were younger.

My kids love to hear stories about when they were little, and they also like to tell stories about things they remember. They also love to hear stories about me and other people in our family when we were little.

Ask your grown-ups to tell you some funny stories about when they were kids or things they were afraid to try but were brave and tried anyway.

Can they also tell you any stories about your grandparents or great grandparents?

Storytelling is a lot of fun and can be a really nice way to start the day as a family.

# TOOL #4: SHORT MORNING MEDITATION

If you remember, one way to think about meditation is noticing your body and your breath. In meditation, you can let your thoughts float past like clouds in the sky. You just notice each thought as it passes.

In the morning, right when you get out of bed, you can find a spot in your room (or make a cozy spot for yourself to have as a meditation space). Take a minute to close your eyes and focus on your deep breath going in through your nose and the big breath coming out through your mouth.

If you want, you can end this breathing with a kind phrase to yourself. Perhaps something like:

> I am loved.

> I am kind.

> I will try my best today.

> I am grateful.

This doesn't have to take a long time (I know your morning is busy). Just see if you can find one minute to meditate and start with that.

# TOOL #5: EVENING: THORN, BUD, ROSE

Every night at dinner, we sit down as a family and ask each other the same questions:

» What is your thorn?

» What is your bud?

» What is your rose?

Thorns can be an ouchie, and we don't like to touch them. When you share your thorn from the day, you are sharing something that you didn't like about your day. Maybe you fell down. Or maybe someone said something to you that hurt your feelings. Perhaps you made a mistake. Sharing your thorn is helpful for your family to hear because they can share about times when they had similar thorns and help you feel better about the things that didn't go so well. That is what family is for—celebrating our accomplishments and helping us when we are feeling sad and things aren't going our way.

A bud on a rose plant is about to turn into a flower. It is excited to open up and share its beauty with the world. When you share your bud at the dinner table, you are sharing something that you are excited about happening in the future.

The rose has already bloomed and is big and beautiful. Your rose from the day is something that went well, something you want to celebrate like the rose celebrates its newly bloomed flower on the stem.

Make the thorn, bud, and rose activity part of each dinner and let it be a new family tradition.

# TOOL #6: EVENING THANKFUL BOX

The last tool I am going to share with you is making a thankful box to use at night.

Find an old shoebox or an extra Amazon box that you have in your house. Decorate the box with markers, stickers, crayons, and cut-out paper.

Cut a slit in the middle of the box where you can put nightly thank-you notes. You can write your note or draw a picture.

Your notes can include something that you are thankful for that has happened in your life already, or they can be about something that you want to be thankful for.

For example, maybe you are worried that you won't learn how to ride your bike, or you won't learn the piano song you have been working so hard to learn. You can give thanks in advance for that already having happened.

You might write, "I am thankful that I will learn how to ride a bike."

Or "I am thankful that I will keep learning my piano song and do well playing it one day."

Being thankful for something that you are worried about can't always make it come true, but it can help take away some of the worries that sometimes come in the evening and help you focus on what is good. Gratitude can also encourage you to keep trying and not give up on your goal.

Learning these tools now will help you so much when you are all grown up, and I want to thank you again for doing these activities and learning the tools in this book.

Here is a special award to celebrate that you and your grown-up have now learned *all these tools*! Yay!

CERTIFICATE

OF COMPLETION

This certificate is Proudly Presented to:

_____

For completing the *Break Free from Reactive Parenting* Book

**LAURA LINN KNIGHT**
AUTHOR & PARENTING EDUCATOR

CERTIFICATE

OF COMPLETION

This certificate is Proudly Presented to:

_____

For completing the *Break Free from Reactive Parenting* Book

**LAURA LINN KNIGHT**
AUTHOR & PARENTING EDUCATOR

I hope you enjoyed learning with me, and remember, if there was a tool or activity that you didn't want to try now, come back to it later.

As you grow, read through your tools again and you will find that your interests may change as you keep growing.

If you did have a favorite tool or you think of some that I should put in my next book, please send me a message on the contact part of my website www.lauralinnknight.com/contact with help from your grown-up. I would love to hear from you!

Big hugs from me to you, my friend.


With love,

Laura

# NOTES

1. "Mothers—and Fathers—Report Mental, Physical Health Declines," March 11, 2021, https://www.apa.org/news/press/releases/stress/2021/one-year-pandemic-stress-parents.

2. A. Rochaun Meadows-Fernandez, "The Mental Health Toll of Parenting During a Pandemic," January 28, 2021, https://www.everydayhealth.com/columns/my-health-story/the-mental-health-toll-of-parenting-during-a-pandemic.

3. Rebecca T. Leeb, "Morbidity and Mortality Weekly Report," November 13, 2020, https://www.cdc.gov/mmwr/volumes/69/wr/mm6945a3.htm.

4. "Children's Mental Health during the COVID-19 Pandemic," May 27, 2021, https://www.luriechildrens.org/en/blog/childrens-mental-health-pandemic-statistics.

5. "Even before COVID-19 Pandemic, Youth Suicide Already at Record High," April 8, 2021, https://health.ucdavis.edu/news/headlines/even-before-covid-19-pandemic-youth-suicide-already-at-record-high/2021/04.

6. You can learn more about mold toxicity in the book *Toxic: Heal Your Body from Mold Toxicity, Lyme Disease, Multiple Chemical Sensitivities, and Chronic Environmental Illness* by Neil Nathan, MD.

7. Oxford English Dictionary, "empathy."

8. Dictionary.com, "fair."

9. Carissa Halston, "Yes, Your Smartphone Habit Is Affecting Your Kid—Here's How," May 11, 2020, https://www.todaysparent.com/family/parenting/yes-your-smartphone-habit-is-affecting-your-kid-heres-how.

10. Crystal Raypole, "How Many Thoughts Do You Have Each Day? And Other Things to Think About," February 22, 2022, https://www.healthline.com/health/how-many-thoughts-per-day#thoughts-per-day.

11. "Why Positive Affirmations Work," May 3, 2020, https://bestself.co/blogs/the-bestself-hub/why-positive-affirmations-work.

12. Catherine Moore, "Positive Daily Affirmations: Is There Science Behind It?" last updated February 14, 2022, https://positivepsychology.com/daily-affirmations.

13. Shreya Gupta, "We Decode the Science Behind Affirmations and How They Can Infuse Positivity in Your Life," May 7, 2021, https://www.healthshots.com/mind/happiness-hacks/we-decode-the-science-behind-affirmations-and-how-they-can-infuse-positivity-in-your-life.

14. "The Science Behind Positive Affirmations," February 14, 2021, https://www.thirdspace.london/this-space/2021/02/the-science-behind-positive-affirmations.

15. Trudi Roth, "The Scientific Power of Positive Affirmations," March 4, 2020, https://further.net/positive-affirmations.

16. Equanimity is mental calmness, composure, and evenness of temper, especially in a difficult situation.

17. Marie Haaland, "Parents Only Spend 24 More Minutes with Their Kids Than Their Phones," October 21, 2019, https://nypost.com/2019/10/21/parents-only-spend -24-more-minutes-with-their-kids-than-their-phones.

18. Jeremy Engle, "Are Your Parents Addicted to Their Phones?" May 30, 2019, https://www.nytimes.com/2019/05/30/learning/are-your-parents-addicted-to-their -phones.html.

19. Denise Ante-Conteras, "Distracted Parenting: How Social Media Affects Parent -Child Attachment," June 2016, https://scholarworks.lib.csusb.edu/cgi/viewcontent .cgi?article=1338&context=etd.

20. AgeEnvyDigital, "Can Smartphone-Addicted Parents Hurt Childhood Development?" January 23, 2020, https://lifeworkscc.com/can-smartphone-addicted -parents-hurt-childhood-development.

21. Katherine Lee, "Why Too Much Cell Phone Usage Can Hurt Your Family Relationships," last updated February 25, 2021, https://www.verywellfamily.com /negative-effects-of-too-much-cell-phone-use-621152.

22. "Parents, Take Note! Smartphone Usage During Family Time May Affect Your Kids' Behaviour," last updated June 14, 2018, https://m.economictimes.com /magazines/panache/parents-take-note-smartphone-usage-during-family-time -may-affect-your-kids-behaviour/articleshow/64588157.cms.

23. Julia Carrie Wong, "Former Facebook Executive: Social Media Is Ripping Society Apart," December 12, 2017, https://amp.theguardian.com/technology/2017/dec/11 /facebook-former-executive-ripping-society-apart.

24. "Screen Addiction Affects Physical and Mental Health," December 9, 2019, https://www.premierhealth.com/your-health/articles/health-topics/screen-addiction -affects-physical-and-mental-health.

25. Indian Institute of Public Health Gandhinagar, "Social Connectedness, Excessive Screen Time during COVID-19 and Mental Health: A Review of Current Evidence," July 22, 2021, https://www.frontiersin.org/articles/10.3389/fhumd.2021.684137/full.

26. Christina Bergmann et al., "Young Children's Screen Time during the First COVID-19 Lockdown in 12 Countries," February 7, 2022, https://www.nature.com /articles/s41598-022-05840-5.

27. "27 Eye-Opening Screen Time Statistics You Should Know," last accessed May 23, 2022, https://www.soocial.com/screen-time-statistics.

28. Derek Thompson, "Why American Teens Are So Sad," April 22, 2022, https:// www.theatlantic.com/newsletters/archive/2022/04/american-teens-sadness -depression-anxiety/629524.

29. Brian Wallace, "Too Much Screen Time Can Harm Your Kids," April 16, 2022, https://gritdaily.com/too-much-screen-time-can-harm-your-kids.

30. Stephanie Pappas, "What Do We Really Know about Kids and Screens?" April 1, 2020, https://www.apa.org/monitor/2020/04/cover-kids-screens.

31. Kait Hanson, "Is 'Squid Game' on Netflix Appropriate for Kids to Watch?" October 14, 2021, https://www.today.com/parents/squid-game-netflix-appropriate -kids-watch-t234372.

32. Beth Ann Mayer, "Kids Are Playing 'Squid Game' at School—Should Parents Be Concerned?" https://www.parents.com/news/kids-playing-squid-game-at-school.

33. Kait Hanson, "What Is Omegle? What Parents Need to Know About Keeping Kids Safe Online," November 8, 2021, https://www.today.com/parents/what-omegle -why-are-children-it-t236335.

34. Nicole Harris, "Is Omegle Safe for Kids? 7 Huge Red Flags for Parents," April 7, 2021, https://www.parents.com/kids/safety/internet/is-omegle-safe-for-kids.

35. Marcy Gordon and Barbara Ortutay, "Ex-Facebook Manager Criticizes Company, Urges More Oversight," October 5, 2021, https://apnews.com/article/facebook -haugen-congress-testimony-1daac7a76ca7bf0b0802cc46e732b51b.

36. Jane Nelsen, "Listen," last accessed May 24, 2022, https://www.positivediscipline .com/articles/listen.

37. Laura Markham, "How to Get Your Child to LISTEN!" last accessed May 24, 2022, https://www.ahaparenting.com/read/How-get-kid-listen.

38. Jon Kabat-Zinn is the founder of the Center for Mindfulness in Medicine, Health Care, and Society (1995), and the Stress Reduction Clinic (1979). He is also the author of several books, including *Full Catastrophe Living*.

39. Elizabeth A. Hofe et al, "Randomized Controlled Trial of Mindfulness Meditation for Generalized Anxiety Disorder: Effects on Anxiety and Stress Reactivity," *Journal of Clinical Psychiatry* 74, no. 8 (August 2013) 786–92, https://pubmed.ncbi .nlm.nih.gov/23541163.

40. Stacy Lu, "Mindfulness Holds Promise for Treating Depression," March 2015, https://www.apa.org/monitor/2015/03/cover-mindfulness.

41. Jeena Cho, "6 Scientifically Proven Benefits of Mindfulness and Meditation," July 14, 2016, "https://www.forbes.com/sites/jeenacho/2016/07/14/10-scientifically- proven-benefits-of-mindfulness-and-meditation/?sh=48aae06663ce.

42. Fadel Zeidan et al, "Mindfulness Meditation Improves Cognition: Evidence of Brief Mental Training," *Consciousness and Cognition* 19, no. 2 (July 2010): 597–605, https://pubmed.ncbi.nlm.nih.gov/20363650.

43. Yi-Yuan, Rongxiang Tang, and Michael I. Posner, "Mindfulness Meditation Improves Emotion Regulation and Reduces Drug Abuse," *Drug and Alcohol Dependence,* June 1, 2016, https://pubmed.ncbi.nlm.nih.gov/27306725.

# ACKNOWLEDGMENTS

I have the honor of writing a parenting book because of my own two children, Oliver and Grace, who have given me the gift of being their mother.

Thank you, Oliver, for sharing this dream with me as we would drive in the car and chat about what tools you found useful and what ideas I could share with the other parents and kids. Thank you, Grace, for being the first one to always try one of my solutions for your big feelings, for cheering me on when I was nervous to share my teachings, and for giving the best hugs (my number one favorite parenting tool).

I would also like to acknowledge my husband, Tyler, for listening to this book time and time again as I wrote each draft. Honey, you have been my biggest supporter since day one and I am so grateful for your encouragement around this book.

And where would I be without my own parents and stepmother, Kathy Wilcox and Steve and Ching Kogan? To my amazing mama, Kathy, thank you for raising me with a love of nature, a traveling spirit, and the belief that anything is possible when you work hard and don't give up. Mama, you are truly always here for me. You have been such a wonderful guide in my life, and I get to be the parent I am today because of you. Thank you! To my father and stepmother, Steve and Ching, I would like to acknowledge your kind words throughout this process, your joy when I told you about this book, and your continued love and support of me, Tyler, and your grand-children. Thank you for being such good parents and grandparents. We love you!

Lastly, I would like to give a special thank-you to my grandmother, Judy Jarvis. Many years ago, when I became interested in becoming a writer, my grandmother and grandfather, Edward, would clip out articles from the newspaper about publishing books and send them to me as encouragement. They always showed true excitement for me as a writer and believed in what I was doing. As my grandmother ages, she is less able to understand the meaningful impact this book will have, but she was there when the idea was born, and I always told myself that I would be sure to dedicate a book to her one day. I am glad the day is upon us, and Grandma, you are a bright light in our family. Thank you for all your unconditional love throughout my life.

Ultimately, I wouldn't have been able to write this book if it were not for all the children I have taught over the years and the families I have worked with. Thank you for having faith in my work and allowing me to be a teacher, a mentor, and a friend.

I hope that *Break Free from Reactive Parenting* will inspire a new model of parenting that allows us to stop old parenting cycles that no longer serve us and raise children with tools and support that will last for generations to come.

Thank you for reading this book. I wish you, dear reader, continued joy on your parenting path.

# ABOUT THE AUTHOR

Laura Linn Knight is a parenting educator, author, mindfulness and meditation leader, mother of two, and former elementary school teacher who helps families create a healthy and calm home. Laura's work has been featured on NBC's *Today Show*, Romper, PureWow, Motherly, *Good Day LA*, and various other media outlets. To learn more, visit www.lauralinnknight.com.